Careering Upwards

Where to find *Right Way*

Elliot *Right Way* take pride in our editorial quality, accuracy and value-for-money. Booksellers everywhere can rapidly obtain any *Right Way* book for you. If you have been particularly pleased with any one title, do please mention this to your bookseller as personal recommendation helps us enormously.

Please send to the address on the back of the title page opposite, a stamped, self-addressed envelope if you would like a copy of our *free catalogue*. Alternatively, you may wish to browse through our extensive range of informative titles arranged by subject on the Internet at **www.right-way.co.uk**

We welcome views and suggestions from readers as well as from prospective authors; do please write to us or e-mail: **info@right-way.co.uk**

Careering Upwards

The Definitive Job-Seeker's Guide to the Selection Process

by

Pauline Grant
MA MSc CPsychol

Typeset in 11/12pt Legacy Serif Book by Letterpart Ltd., Reigate, Surrey.

Printed and bound in Great Britain by Guernsey Press Co. Ltd., Guernsey, Channel Islands.

The *Right Way Plus* series is published by Elliot Right Way Books, Brighton Road, Lower Kingswood, Tadworth, Surrey, KT20 6TD, U.K. For information about our company and the other books we publish, visit our web site at www.right-way.co.uk

Contents

Dedication

This book was informed by my work and conversations with clients and the job-seekers who shared their experiences with me. I couldn't have written it without them, together with the encouragement of friends and colleagues at YSC Ltd. I gratefully acknowledge them as stimulants, contributors and shapers. For me, the hardest work was at the end, when I received the proofs. This was when Jonathan's support was invaluable. In recognition of that most subtle yet potent of motivators, the unshakeable belief of the best of friends, I dedicate this to Viv.

Pauline Grant

Introduction

If you are one of the many people on the job market, or thinking of putting yourself there, this book is aimed directly at you!

Apart from people who are out of work and want to be back in, there are many people in positions that really don't suit them. For whatever reason, they have found that the kind of work they are doing is not stimulating, or they lack opportunities to progress, or maybe the work is fine but the organisation fails to provide the right environment. If you are one of these people, you want to be sure that your next career step is a better one.

Perhaps this is your first move into the job market, or maybe it has been some time since you last applied for a new position. The process by which organisations currently make their choices between candidates may be unfamiliar to you, and you want to be prepared to do your best. It may surprise you to know that the organisations you are applying to share your aspiration *that you do your best at their selection process*. They also want the people they select to be enthusiastic about the opportunity they are offering. For them, getting the right people is at least as important as having the right strategy and making the right investment decision; in fact, recruiting is a form of investment.

So both you and the organisations you are applying to have something in common. Both parties want to make the right decision. You want your next job to be right for you, and they want to find people who can take them forward. They also have to take account of the diversity of people who could add value to their organisation, and ensure that they are not excluding people unfairly. The wrong selection decision is costly to organisations. It means that they have to go through the whole process again much sooner than they anticipated, or that they fail to obtain the benefits of getting the best person in the right job.

To avoid making the wrong selection decisions, most organisations have adopted more rigorous and comprehensive selection procedures. They have made efforts to concentrate on the qualities and characteristics that are important for success in their organisation, and to be objective in their decisions about candidates. They use more structure in their interviews. They often include other kinds of assessment exercises to help them uncover candidates' strengths, and of course to reveal limitations. You will find many of these techniques in the following chapters.

Selection involves scrutiny. Whenever you are closely observed, there are potential opportunities for you to learn more about yourself: what skills and characteristics other people value, and what impact you make on them. This can lead to deeper self-insight, and therefore provides the basis for developing yourself. Some pointers on how to make the most of these opportunities have also been included.

Of course, the assumption is that you have already jumped the first hurdle; you have made an application that has not been rejected, and you have been invited to take part in the next stage of the selection process. However, if you are having some difficulties, there is some guidance towards the end of the book to help you tune your search strategy.

Throughout the book you will find that your time is considered to be a valuable resource. You want to target this resource well and to make sure that you are not wasting it. Hopefully by the end you will be more focused on the jobs that you really want, that play closely to your strengths and that provide a working environment in which you can flourish. Since that is what your employer wants too, the result should be a win-win!

Chapter 1:

What Are You Looking For?

It has been said that looking for a job can seem like a full-time job in itself, that it's a "numbers game" and that the more chances you give yourself, the better. Whether you are currently unemployed, in a job that no longer suits you or just ready for a change, finding a new job usually takes real work and you may have to put a lot of time and effort into securing a suitable position. Every letter you write or interview you attend can be thought of as using up some of your total resource of time and energy. This chapter is about seeing that time and effort as an investment.

Best Use of Your Time

When attending one interview you can't at the same time be attending another, or indeed be doing something else productive with your time. So each occasion carries an "opportunity cost" - you lose an opportunity to be doing something else that might be more effective use of your time. It is therefore important to focus your resource - your time. This means making conscious decisions about the organisations you target and the positions you put time and effort into pursuing.

Your time is important, and so is the time of the organisations you are applying to. As well as wanting to make sure that you don't waste your time, it might be worth thinking about the impact on a potential employer if you present yourself as a candidate when you are not really interested in the job, or not able to meet its demands. There may come a time in the future when the same organisation is offering a position that would really suit you, and where you have the necessary skills. You don't want to be ruled out for that because you have been seen as a time-waster in the past.

Considering the "Fit"

There are very good and obvious reasons for concentrating on the jobs where you have the necessary skills and experience. However, it may not be so obvious that you can also make choices about the organisations that are likely to work in a way that suits your personal style and offer the opportunities that line up with your aspirations.

For example, let's say you are the sort of person who is a steady worker, not particularly ambitious. Perhaps the important thing for you is to be allowed to do a good job without being pushed to take on additional responsibilities. You might be very unhappy in a company that puts pressure on you to do more than you feel able to do, perhaps because you want to devote some of your energies elsewhere. After a time, you might resent this and feel that your work was not being valued. Your motivation could suffer and, even if you could, you might not put in the extra effort that was being called for. This could lead to your being criticised which in turn could make you even more de-motivated. You might try hard for a while, and then start to be dissatisfied because you no longer had time for other interests.

Maybe you are a very sociable individual who enjoys a lot of contact with other people. You might be faced with a dilemma if you went to an interview knowing that the job you were applying for required you to work for long periods on your own. Do you bluff your way through and try to pretend that you really don't mind if you don't speak to another human being all day? Or, when asked, do you admit that you'd find this dull, with the strong possibility that you would be rejected?

Throughout this book you will find that you are never encouraged to bluff! This is on pragmatic as well as moral grounds. Firstly, it can be difficult to sustain bluffing through a structured assessment process, and, if you come across as less than genuine, you will immediately reduce

"Oh no, there goes my golf handicap."

You start to be dissatisfied because you no longer have time for other interests.

your chances of being successful. Secondly, if you are one of the rare people who can bluff well and can maintain it long enough to get the job, the chances are that you will be unhappy, whereas if you found a position that suits your style more closely you would gain more satisfaction. Thirdly, and this might appear to be a more subtle point, job hunting can be a difficult enough experience, carrying as it does the possibility of repeated rejection; what does it do for your self-esteem if you convince yourself that you have to lie to be acceptable?

The perfect position for you might not exist. Most of us have to make compromises to achieve a lifestyle that is broadly speaking acceptable. Making a positive choice about what you will compromise leaves you feeling in control of your own destiny, and for most people this is an important component of their overall job satisfaction. Let's say you have the opportunity of taking a job that pays well, but means that you have to make a long journey each day. Some people would prefer to have more money and would therefore be prepared to endure the long journey. However, others would be prepared to sacrifice some salary for more time to do other things. Knowing what is important to you personally is an important part of making this kind of choice. A "good fit" can be thought of as the result when:

- Your skills, experience, personal style and abilities are very close to what is required to do the job - any gap is known in advance and there is a way of addressing it.
- The working environment provides most of what you need to have a satisfying working life - any mis-match is acknowledged and you have made a positive decision about where you are prepared to compromise.

The working environment has some visible and tangible features, such as:

- The location and surroundings.
- The pay and other benefits.
- The resources and facilities you have at your disposal.

It also has some less tangible features, including:

- The kind of people you will be working with.
- The behaviours and characteristics that are valued.
- The social "feel" of your workplace or team.
- How people are rewarded aside from pay.
- The organisational values.

The rest of this chapter concentrates on assessing yourself and using this information to help define the ideal working environment for you. In this way you can make decisions about the opportunities to which you want to give higher priority, and where you are prepared to make compromises.

Taking Stock of Yourself

Let's start with you. What do you have on offer? Taking stock of your strengths and preferences will give you a good idea of what you have to offer an employer. By thinking about these in advance you will have more chance of bringing them to mind when involved in a selection process. To make this exercise most useful to you, try to think of examples that illustrate the skills or characteristics you have identified. You are likely to find that listing these is not a "one-off" task, but rather a picture that you can build up over a length of time by periodically returning to your list and adding to it. Reading through it before attending an interview or selection process will remind you of what you have to offer.

Technical Skills and Qualifications - Expertise gained through study or apprenticeship, verified by certificates or a record of success in applying the skills. Remember to include everything that might be relevant - even if it is not specifically asked for. For instance:

- Are you more than averagely computer literate or do you have excellent keyboard speed?
- Can you converse in another language or translate?
- Do you have specific academic or technical qualifications?
- Have you taken courses that relate to a business function, such as sales, finance or logistics?
- Are there more general work skills you have, such as project management?
- Can you put together a presentation using the latest audio-visual aids?

Experience - that could add to your flexibility and value to a company; things you have done at or outside work that demonstrate abilities in addition to those for which you have qualifications. For instance:

- Have you led teams, departments or projects?
- Have you successfully held leadership or organisational roles, perhaps outside work such as the cadets, school governor, club treasurer?
- Do you possess good coaching skills so that you can help others learn? Have you acted as a mentor to new entrants?
- Have you organised outings, conferences or events?
- Do people see you as someone to consult when they have problems?
- Have you been involved in making substantial changes, such as introducing new processes or re-locating a head office?

Personal Characteristics - that contribute to the workplace. Trawl your sources of information. For instance:

- Have you had feedback from previous colleagues or your manager, either formally or informally? What did this tell you about your personal characteristics?
- What do your friends say about you? Which characteristics do they appreciate?
- Have you completed personality questionnaires and discussed your profile?
- How do you respond when you meet new people, and how do they react to you?
- What do you value in other people? Are they the characteristics that are similar to your own, or different?
- How organised, diligent and thorough are you in general?
- How imaginative, resourceful and adventurous are you?
- What kinds of activities interest you and sustain your attention?

- How do you respond to criticism, disappointment and uncertainty?
- How quickly do you bounce back when things go wrong?

Using feedback and your experience of how you respond, you can construct a summary of your personal characteristics, together with a comment about how they make you more valuable to an employer. (Chapter 5 on Personality Tests might help to prompt your thinking.)

Here are some examples of how personal characteristics can be an added resource:

"I'm a sociable person who gets on with people easily. I can build good working relationships quickly."

"People say I'm kind-hearted, and that I usually notice when someone is feeling down. I'd be caring and sympathetic to other people at work."

"I'm known as a helpful person. Everyone knows that if there's a problem I'm the one who will help sort it out. I'll offer as well – not wait to be asked."

"I've had feedback that I'm very reliable and always meet deadlines. I'd never promise to do something unless I knew I could deliver."

"Previous colleagues have often said I'm fun to work with, and that this helps when the pressure's on."

"I know I tend to be pessimistic, but this is often an asset as I'll spot the potential problems that other people might overlook."

"I get bored by routine, so I'm always looking for ways of making the job more interesting – mainly for myself, but it also works for other people."

Things that Motivate You - the things that you will work for and which make up the environment that best suits you. For instance:

- What are your longer term aspirations? What kind of lifestyle do you aspire to? How ambitious are you?
- Where have you been happiest/least happy? What does this tell you about what affects your job satisfaction?
- What is important to you in terms of reward, apart from money - such as status, recognition or seeing tangible results? How do these things rank against money in terms of importance to you?
- How far are you prepared to take risks, move house or travel?
- What persuades you to do something that is difficult?
- What support do you draw on when you feel down or uncertain?
- How do you set your own objectives and direction? Do you like to have clear life goals or do you prefer to let things happen and wait for opportunities?
- How important are other people in your life?
- What is your attitude to change?
- Under what circumstances do you learn most easily?
- What frustrates or irritates you?
- How much time do you like to spend on non-work activities? How important to you are your outside interests?

Most people are able to highlight a few things that are really important to them and that would affect their choice of employment. Sometimes these factors are strongly held beliefs, and the people holding them would not compromise them at any cost. Examples might be those people who were so committed to animal rights that they would not work in an industry that they thought exploited or abused animals, or people who were determined to work for an environmentally responsible employer. Another example is the level of pay. There might be a figure below which you could not accept a job offer. This might be because you need that level of income to maintain your lifestyle and are not prepared to adjust to a lower level of spending. It could also be that you have a clear idea of your "worth" and would find it humiliating to work for less.

These factors are sometimes referred to as "hygiene" factors – they are necessary as far as you are concerned, and whilst their presence does not add to your satisfaction, their absence would significantly detract. These are the things you *need to have.*

However, many things are less clear cut. You might prefer to have a lot of variety in your work, but be prepared to take something with a lot of routine activities as long as your work pattern left you enough time to get your variety outside of work. You might want to work for a "blue chip" organisation because you like the prestige, but know that you could get a more senior position in a less well-known company – you would have to decide which was more important to you. These are *nice to have* factors – you want some of them, but would not need all of them.

Then there are factors that make you want to put in extra effort. Maybe you are motivated by being appreciated and having your efforts acknowledged. If someone encourages you, maybe this makes you more able to take risks or try new things. Perhaps you like to know that you are being helpful, and, if someone needs you, this will make you work even harder. You might be very competitive and want to be the top performer. These factors are the ones that really motivate you. Unlike the hygiene factors, a bit more of these will have a pronounced effect on your job satisfaction. By identifying these, you will be on the way to defining the kind of working environment that is likely to get the best performance from you, and to make you feel good at the same time.

Describing your Ideal Working Environment

From the information you have compiled, you are now in a position to construct your ideal working environment. Of course the real world is seldom a good match for the ideal, but, by being clear about what suits you best, you are also in a good position to make choices about where you will compromise.

Here are some examples to give you an idea of how to describe your ideal working environment:

Your ideal working environment.

Example 1

"The ideal would be where I had a boss who trusted me and let me make my own decisions, but made regular times to touch base with me. I'd have colleagues to talk things through with, and we could be very open with each other. We would socialise together often. The work could be demanding – I would be prepared to put in long hours – but no-one would question me if I wanted to take an afternoon

off. There would be opportunities for travel, maybe two or three times a year. I'd be encouraged to learn new skills and to make sure I kept at the 'cutting edge'. The company would have room for me to grow and be promoted – I'd be expected to be accountable for my decisions and prepared to stand or fall by them. They would allow me to try out new things and, within limits, not punish me if it didn't work out. They would accept my odd sense of humour and tolerate my occasional lack of tact."

Example 2

"My ideal working environment would be steady and structured. I don't like surprises, so I'd want to know what was likely to happen in the future. My working hours would be predictable so that I could continue with outside commitments. I wouldn't want work to encroach on my private life. I'd be prepared to move at the right time, but for the next couple of years I don't want to uproot my family. I need some security. I'd be happy to be trained in new areas. I want to have a team to manage because I'm good at getting the best out of other people. I accept that some of them would overtake me, so I need a place where I can progress at my own pace and not be seen as a blocker. Equally I don't want to be prevented from making progress because of my age. I can work to deadlines as long as I'm clear about what the priorities are. I've worked from an office and with open plan – open plan is probably best for me because it gives me opportunities to find out what's going on elsewhere, and I am quite reserved."

Example 3

"I like the flexibility to plan my own activities and to work when I want to. I sometimes choose to work at weekends and take time off in the week, so ideally this would be acceptable. I need the buzz of creative people to stimulate my thinking. I can be very spontaneous, and should work with someone who is more practical and can finish things off. Good administrative support is vital as I often leave things to the last minute. I don't need any of the corporate

trappings – health insurance, car, pension – but I expect a high income and would prefer it to be performance related. I know I'm good at motivating people, but I can also be very tough on them, so I'd work best with a company that has a culture of excellence."

As you can see from these examples, different things are important to different people. Not getting everything you want is a likely reality, but you should be clear about when you are making compromises. It's often easier to live with them if we have chosen to do so rather than found that we have to! For instance, the person in Example 2 may find that in a particular company only younger managers have a real prospect of reaching senior positions, so this person might have to compromise his ambitions in that organisation. However, he may decide that this is a positive trade off for some security and stable working hours. The person in Example 3 may be prepared to be more constrained in terms of when she works, but knows that without good back-up she is unlikely to be successful, so might not find it acceptable if she has no say in who provides the administrative support.

Compromising Positively – The Selection Process

By now you have thought about yourself and what you have to offer. You have also thought about the organisation and what an ideal working environment might look like. Being realistic, you might make some compromises when it comes to looking at a specific opportunity. However, this leaves the issue of how to deal with questions in a selection process that concentrate on the areas where you know there is a compromise to be made.

I have already covered why it is important to make these compromises positively and cautioned against bluffing. A more productive and self-affirming way of approaching the task of finding a job is to know yourself very well, and accept your deficiencies as well as your abilities and strengths. You need a way of presenting yourself honestly that, at the same time, shows that you are an attractive candidate.

Let's take the example of someone who likes being around other people and yet still decides to pursue an opportunity that means working in virtual solitude.

A legitimate question during the selection process might be "How do you feel about working on your own?" Now consider the following possible responses:

1. "I think I'll be fine. I like my own company and I prefer to get on with what I'm doing without being interrupted."
2. "I don't know. I've never been in that position before. I'm used to having other people around to chat to – it helps to pass the time."
3. "I'm sure I'll find it hard at first because I enjoy company. I'd have to make sure I worked really hard in short bursts so that I could make time to go and have a chat from time to time."

The first response might be seen as ideal, as it would be if it were true. But our candidate is just trying to create a good impression. This can be a mistake, as responses to other questions or behaviour in other parts of the selection process are likely to raise doubts. An employer will be put off by candidates who dissemble. This candidate would also fail to demonstrate that the motivational implications of the work situation had been considered.

The second response is at least honest, but would not fill the interviewer with confidence! The third shows the same honesty, but adds to it some additional insight. The person here is showing an understanding of the difficulty and has given some thought to how it could be dealt with. In this way, what might be seen as a deficiency relative to a particular job can be put in a more positive light.

Of course, if you had identified a deficiency such as this, and no matter how hard you tried to work round it, you still felt that it would present a problem for you, you have a different decision to make. Do you go along to the selection process nevertheless or do you withdraw? This might be the time when you decide to withdraw as you are very unlikely to be successful. Or, if you were successful in getting the job, you would only take it if nothing else came up - and you might end up hating it!

The more you can think through these decisions in advance, the more likely you are to avoid wasting your time and the time of the prospective employer.

Pulling it All Together

Having done some thinking about yourself, you can now pull this together by constructing answers to the following questions:

- What do I have to offer employers that makes me attractive to them, now and in the future? (Remember to include personal characteristics as well as skills, qualifications and experience.)
- What are the things that are really important to me that would need to be present for me to take a job - the things I would not be prepared to do without? (These are the "hygiene" factors - the *need to have*.)
- What other things are important to me, but I would be prepared to compromise as long as other things compensated? (These are the *nice to have* - where you would compromise on some, but not all.)
- What additional things should I look for that really motivate me? (These are the factors that will significantly increase your job satisfaction and help you to perform at your best.)
- If I decide to compromise, how can I present this in a positive way for an employer? (This shows that you understand the implications of taking a job where the situation is not ideal.)

Summary

This chapter has concentrated on helping you to look at all the things that will affect your job satisfaction and make you attractive to an employer. The objective is to save you from wasting time - your time and that of the organisations you are applying to. There is no point in attending interviews where you have no chance of success; and you will want to be sure with the more marginal ones that you can feel positively about presenting yourself.

Being very honest with yourself about what you want and what you have to offer an employer will assist you in preparing for interview and being confident. ("Doing your best" is covered later in the book.) But it will also help you to select yourself out and thereby focus your attention on the more likely prospects. This filtering down process should make you feel more realistically optimistic about the opportunities you do decide to pursue.

Finding out about the company will tell you more about the likely fit between your characteristics and those that are valued and rewarded in that organisation. Even if you have the technical requirements for the job, you might find the company is too different from the environment that best suits you. This is covered in the next chapters.

Chapter 2:

What Companies Are Looking For

In this chapter we try to look at things from the point of view of the prospective employer. There will be a reason behind the design of any selection event, and by getting an understanding of the kinds of things that are important to the employer you are better placed to present yourself well. You also need to be realistic about the time you put into each opportunity that you pursue. If you are unlikely to meet the company's requirements, you may prefer to concentrate your efforts elsewhere.

The Job Description

The design of a selection process will usually start with a description of what is required in the job, and when you apply for a position you may receive some kind of job description. The chances are that what you get is a summary of a more detailed version that has been drawn up within the company. The job title is often a good guide, but not always - you need to know about the company hierarchy to judge whether a title of "manager" carries more responsibility than "controller" for instance.

The job description should give information about the size of the role - such as the budget you would be in charge of, the number of people who would report to you or the scope of your activities.

Job Description – Head of Credit Management

Reports to Finance Director

Main Purpose
To contribute to the development and implementation of a plan that delivers the strategic objectives of the Division:
- Ensuring that Credit Risk is controlled and managed for optimal profitability.
- Lending Policy.
- Portfolio Measurement.

The Job-holder must ensure that:
- Credit policy is consistent and effectively applied.
- Credit is properly controlled and balanced with profitability.
- Key processes and credit assessment techniques in the Division are first class.

Authority
Credit management of £3500m pa of new business.
Cost budget of £1.3m.
Lending mandate £500k. Payment Approval mandate £500k.

Key Internal Relationships
New Mortgage Lending. Existing Portfolios.

Key External Relationships
Credit Scoring Consultants. Credit Rating Agencies.
Fraud Prevention Agencies.

Main Accountabilities
1. Control of credit risk over all existing lending and future business.
2. Compliance of all credit aspects of lending with legislation and industry regulations.
3. The development of effective Management Information.
4. First-class new-business processes that deliver efficient cost-effective services to customers.
5. Develop automated decision-making systems to achieve cost efficiencies in the lending process.
6. Administration of lending policy (e.g. authorities and exposure limits) to ensure prudent lending.
7. Represent Credit Management at Lending Policy committee and provide secretarial support to the committee, ensuring that meetings are well attended, promised deliverables are made and deadlines are achieved.

Fig. 1. Job Description – Head of Credit Management.

MARKETING DIRECTOR, EASTERN EUROPE – Job Description

Reporting to the MD of ABC Eastern Europe, the Marketing Director is a board level position.
A 2–3 year assignment is envisaged.

Key Accountabilities

- Working with the board, develop and implement brand strategies to grow market share profitably, specifically:
    1. Develop programmes to establish ABC profile and brand leadership.
    2. Open new markets through acquired businesses.
    3. Expand the franchise.
- Brand direction to colleagues in export development.
- Lead new product development initiatives.
- Provide strategic leadership, training and development to marketing department.

Fig. 2. Job Description – Marketing Director.

ORGANISATION & MANAGEMENT DEVELOPMENT MANAGER – reporting to the HR Director

Key Outputs

- Deliver business unit strategy for OD.
- Lead and facilitate succession planning.
- Review organisation structures.
- Create development plans.
- Define capability standards and coach/train managers in effective selection and people judgments.

Fig. 3. Job Description – Organisation & Management Development Manager.

JOB TITLE: Shift Team Leader (STL)

Reports To: Shift Manager (SM)

Job Purpose

The Shift Team Leader is responsible for the supervision of a production area whilst on shift. Meeting targets of output, quality and delivery to an agreed cost within the production area is the primary role. The STL will also be responsible for liaising with manufacturing support functions while on shift.

Key Accountabilities

Planning: Agreeing the daily plan for the production line/facility with the shift planner.

Goals: Communicating the daily targets to the operators on shift.

Overtime: Using overtime budget selectively to achieve the plan.

Correction: Applying corrective procedures to redress any shortfalls as they arise.

Teamwork: Promote an environment where operators work jointly to achieve objectives and set challenging targets.

Output: To achieve the agreed shift target for output on a daily basis.

Quality: To produce agreed levels of saleable product at all times.

Discipline: Applying company rules for performance, conduct, absenteeism and lateness.

Housekeeping: Keeping the production area neat and tidy at all times.

Succession Planning: Ensuring STL cover by deputies and also standing in for SM as required.

Production Skills: Developing production skills and knowledge in every production area.

Key Performance Indicators

Output: Meet planned output daily (+/-5% target).

Quality: Meet the agreed quality target every day.

Planning: Meet the adherence to plan target every day.

Delivery: Achieve agreed production target every day.

Changeovers: Meet agreed changeover targets.

Overview

The Shift Team Leader (STL) is a senior supervisory role and pivotal to the overall success of the manufacturing unit and the business as a whole.

Fig. 4. Job Description – Shift Team Leader.

The "Person Specification"

Having given thought to the nature of the job, most companies will then translate this into a specification of the kind of person they wish to recruit, and who will be able to be successful in that role. In some cases they will be very systematic about this and use a structured format. One that has been popular for many years is known as Rodgers' 7 Point Plan, after the person who devised it.

The 7 Point Plan is a kind of checklist; a reminder to recruiters to consider each of the seven factors when determining the kind of person they want to employ, and then to assess candidates against each. The factors are:

- **Physical make-up**. This draws attention to the physical requirements of the job. For instance, does it require physical strength to move heavy equipment or a keen sense of smell to distinguish different perfume components?
- **Attainments**. The level of educational qualifications required for the job is the focus here.
- **General intelligence**. Aside from academic qualifications, the job might need a certain level of intellect to deal with complex problems or to give assurance that the candidate will respond to training.
- **Special aptitudes**. The role might require particular talents that are not covered by either of the previous points. Examples here might be IT skills, the ability to pick up languages easily or a facility with numbers. It could also cover the less measurable aptitudes, such as organising or influencing.
- **Interests**. The idea here is that people's interests give an indication of their motivation and drive. Also, some roles demand a level of social interaction or comfort with making new contacts, and interests outside work can indicate whether this is likely to be an issue for candidates.

- **Disposition**. The kind of people who are most likely to be successful will be described here – effectively an idea of what their personality profiles will look like.
- **Circumstances**. Now we are getting to a more practical area. A role might need someone to be away from home a lot, work unsocial hours or relocate to another town.

You can probably see from this list where many current assessment and selection methods come from. Personality tests used in selection are related specifically to "disposition", for example. A standard procedure when a vacancy needs to be filled is for the job description to be reviewed, then a person specification drawn up along the lines of the 7 Point Plan or some similar format, then an advertisement prepared that will attract candidates who are likely to meet the requirements.

Person Specification – Head of Credit Management
A seasoned Credit Management Professional with a strong Credit Scoring background and extensive experience in financial services covering:

- Policy development & implementation.
- Credit systems development.
- Behavioural scoring techniques.
- Introduced and Branch sourced mortgage portfolios.
- Staff organisation and management.

In addition the job holder will demonstrate:

- Excellent written communication skills.
- Attention to detail.
- A credible and persuasive manner.
- IT literacy.

Fig. 5. Person Specification – Head of Credit Management.

Person Specification – Marketing Director

- A forward thinking marketing professional with 10 years of experience in marketing.
- Experience working with fmcg.
- Experience leading professional marketing personnel.
- A strong international orientation. The person must have the flexibility to work with different cultures and environments.
- The person must speak or be willing to learn Russian.
- Strong verbal communication skills.
- The person will be required to work closely with export colleagues and must demonstrate the ability to build working relationships focused on the business.

Fig. 6. Person Specification – Marketing Director.

Person Specification – Shift Team Leader

- Experienced in management and working to agreed targets.
- Adaptability and resilience to deal with a demanding position with a high pace of change.
- Able to make quick decisions to satisfy short term customer needs.
- Ability to work with large numbers of people with different styles.
- Good leadership and team facilitation skills.
- Numerate and articulate.
- Flexible coaching approach; able both to advise and instruct.

Fig. 7. Person Specification – Shift Team Leader.

Person Specification – Organisation & Management Development Manager

Qualifications

- Graduate calibre.
- IPD or post graduate qualification in HR.

Experience

- Min 8 years' experience in HR: 4 within a management development or O & MD role.
- Worked in progressive organisations with strong change orientation.

Skills & Knowledge

- Change Management.
- Relating Business Strategy to HR Strategy.
- Facilitation/Process Design.
- Coaching.
- Organisation Design.
- Development Planning.
- Recruitment and Selection.
- Observation and Assessment.
- Presentation.
- Clear Communication.

Personal Characteristics

- Commercially aware.
- Strategic Thinker.
- Very insightful about people.
- Influential.
- Resilient.

Fig. 8. Person Specification – Organisation & Management Development Manager.

The selection procedure is designed to assess the required characteristics – and, of course, the application form will cover some of these points so that some applicants are screened out and only those who meet the criteria are invited to proceed further.

Organisational Competences

The "7 Point Plan" has been widely used by many organisations when putting together a specification for the type of person who is most likely to be successful in a particular role. However, it looks a little dated now. The reason it looks dated is that there is greater recognition that people change and so do their jobs. If we only look at the requirements of the job of today, we may recruit people who quickly become out of their depth as newer technologies are introduced or more flexible working is required.

"We don't use this any more, but we let her pretend because she has such a sunny disposition."

People quickly become out of their depth as newer technologies are introduced.

Equally, if we are too rigid about a person's current circumstances or level of academic qualification, we can reject people who could easily be trained and who, in time, become more able to make a significant contribution to the company.

Another reason the approach is dated is that it contains some assumptions that are not always valid in practice. For example, we might consider that someone who has achieved a high level of academic performance in a particular subject will also be effective in applying that in a working environment. This gives undue importance to the level of qualification, and does not take enough account of the differences in the situation. Passing an examination is very different from motivating a team, convincing a colleague or briefing an outside agency.

A development has been a move to define the competences, sometimes called competencies, that are central to the company's success. (Examples of these can be found in Chapter 8, The Interview, where we look at one of the ways people are assessed against competences.) A "competence" can be thought of as the outcome when someone uses his or her knowledge, skills and experience to address work issues. Competences are durable because they look at the results rather than defining what lies behind them. An analogy might be with athletes – we would want to see how fast they could run or how high they could jump, rather than whether their training schedules had included lifting weights. By assessing candidates against competences there is more assurance that they will be effective in a real work environment.

You are unlikely to be given a set of competences when you apply for a job. However, you can use your knowledge of the company to consider what you think they would regard as important. Most competence lists cover three areas:

- **Business** – focusing on activities that add value to the business by, for instance, responding to customer requirements, ensuring that initiatives are profitable, defining the strategic direction, managing risk. Even "not for profit" organisations will have goals that relate to service levels and efficiency.

- **Interpersonal** – concentrating on the interactions with other people, such as building successful teams, collaborating cross-functionally, showing leadership by motivating and developing people. Sometimes this will extend to relationships outside the company, such as with suppliers or industry organisations.
- **Individual** – relating to the personal qualities that lead to success, such as resilience, personal impact, being organised and meeting deadlines or showing enthusiasm.

As competences are usually for the organisation as a whole, they will be supplemented in a selection assessment by the specific functional or technical expertise demanded by the job. However, someone who is technically expert but who does not meet the other competence requirements is unlikely to be successful.

A New "7" – The Seven Signs of Success

One of the things that has changed in recent years is the unwritten or "psychological" contract between employer and employee. In the past it was generally assumed that loyalty would be rewarded by security, and that there was a kind of paternalistic relationship between an employing organisation and the people who worked there. The degree to which this has changed will vary from company to company, but most would now see people's wish to progress and develop as a natural consequence of their ambitions and abilities. If you have reached the limit in one company, but have the potential to go further, it makes sense to look elsewhere.

Whereas in the past people might have been wary of letting their employer know they were looking for other opportunities, many are now more relaxed about having a career discussion that might result in the decision to pursue their aspirations elsewhere. Indeed, some companies would encourage people to think broadly about their career progression and support them by making sure that the exit was a satisfactory one. Whilst this might seem odd at first, it is also mature and forward thinking. Very able people might one day wish to return in a more senior role having gained valuable experience elsewhere, so letting them go in a positive way can be a worthwhile investment. This is very different from the days when even thinking about leaving the company would be seen as a kind of treason!

Very able people might one day wish to return in a more senior role.

The trend is more towards individuals seeing themselves as a marketable asset, and organisations acquiring or disposing of those assets as required by the business imperatives at the time. This can be seen as a realistic response to a changing environment. However, it also has consequences in terms of security – people generally are deluding themselves if they feel that they have a job for life, or if they believe that they are indispensable.

When organisations are putting together their "specification" for the person they want to employ now, they are more likely to concentrate on the current situation and the foreseeable future when thinking about the skills and experience. They might therefore be more tolerant of characteristics that are not central to successful performance, but less flexible about those that get in the way of making an immediate impact. Longer term careers are built more on shared values than specific skills, so these are likely to take on greater importance. In the employment market of the future, what are the themes that might contribute to this specification? The "seven signs of success" might be:

- **Track record.** It is a fairly obvious fact, backed up by research findings, that the past is a good predictor of the future. People who have already demonstrated success in a particular area are likely to be able to repeat that success. Of course there will always be some differences between the situation they were in *then* and the situation in the present company *now*. However, where these differences are incremental rather than substantial, track record is a good indication of how people are likely to perform. The company might also be on the lookout for people who have very specific experience, for instance in implementing a new system, re-locating a head office or launching an innovative product. If the candidate has a proven track record, this will give the employing company confidence.

- **Benchmarking.** Successful organisations have a keen awareness of where they sit in relation to other similar organisations. They will therefore be especially attracted to candidates who can bring experience from a company that is just ahead of them in some way. Even if the candidate does not have this experience, the knowledge of what "good" looks like, what constitutes excellence, will be valued. This might be in relation to a particular market, process or environment. Where organisations are already leaders in a particular field, they will be on the lookout for someone who can keep them there, for instance by being innovative. What they will avoid is bringing in someone from outside the company who adds no more value than someone already employed. It costs less to recruit internally, so there has to be a reason for taking an external candidate.
- **Values.** Where the recruitment is at an early stage in the person's career, there may be little track record or experience to go on. A person's values will therefore be an important indicator as to how he or she is likely to fit in with the organisation. This is also significant for any recruit. The degree to which the candidate holds values that are in line with that of the organisation is a key factor in recruitment decisions. A misfit in terms of values is likely to be regarded as a contra-indication when it comes to making a selection decision, even if the capabilities are present to do the job. An organisation's values are central to its culture, and someone who is uncomfortable with the beliefs that are important to the company, or who is opposed to them, is unlikely to have much of a future there. Where a company has re-defined its values, it will be even more important to them to recruit people who are staunch supporters and who can help to embed the new culture.
- **Credibility.** Most jobs require people to work together in some way and many will depend on being able to

influence other people. Credibility will be measured in terms of how likely the candidates are to be able to make an impact with the people they have to work with and influence them appropriately. Even very able people will fail in their role if they cannot persuade other people to follow them, support them or co-operate with them. In some roles this will extend to being credible with some groups outside the company. Dealing with investors, the media, industry regulators or government think tanks are all examples where this is important.

- **Flexibility.** Change is so much a part of everyday working life that many people find that the job they are doing is markedly different from the one they were initially recruited to do. That might be the result of re-organisation of roles and responsibilities, or developments in technology, or in response to changing market dynamics. Or the company might be recruiting someone with a view to filling a more senior role in the future. Being able to adapt, learn, work with different kinds of people and adjust to different environments might be as important as skills and experience.
- **Holistic approach.** Having the maturity to look beyond personal objectives and see the impact on the business as a whole can be important at every level in an organisation. Having a clear understanding of why one's role is important to the business and how it fits in with other roles often contributes to a person's success. Continuous improvement demands that people look beyond their own job and collaborate with other functions to ensure that processes are efficient and are beneficial to the organisation. People who just want to do their own job and are not sensitive to the links with the jobs of other people may find that they are considered something of a dinosaur.
- **Receptiveness to learning.** Keeping up to date and ensuring skills are continually refreshed demands that

a person is keen to keep learning. There might be an intellectual component to this in terms of being able to respond to training, but it also includes having the curiosity and open-mindedness to acknowledge one's own limitations. There will be few areas where people can say that they know enough and need no further development. Even if they are at the leading edge in terms of their skill, they might need to become better at teamwork, leadership or coaching others. People who come across as complacent or arrogant are less likely to be attractive candidates.

Summary – Getting Down to Specifics

Now that you have had an overview of what organisations in general are likely to be looking for, you can start to focus on the more specific things that are relevant to your application. The next chapter looks at how you can do this by finding out about the company. When doing your research, keep in mind the three competence areas:

- Business.
- Interpersonal.
- Individual.

Also remember the seven signs of success:

- Track record.
- Benchmarking.
- Values.
- Credibility.
- Flexibility.
- Holistic approach.
- Receptiveness to learning.

Try to build up a picture of what the organisation might be looking for. The next stage will be to assess yourself, as well as you can, against these requirements.

Chapter 3:

Finding Out About The Company

When you apply for a position with a particular company or organisation, you may already know something about them. Perhaps you are a consumer of their products or a user of their services. Maybe it's an organisation that has attracted a lot of publicity so you've seen them mentioned in the press. It may be that you know someone who used to work for one of their competitors. All these give you clues as to how to find out more about the organisation.

In this chapter we'll be looking at how to increase your knowledge of the organisation before you decide whether or not you want to work for them. There are good reasons for doing this. If you attend a selection event, you want to be sure that you are not wasting your time. You will probably be spending several hours with them, and if you could be spending that time more productively applying for positions that suit you better, this can be very costly! Also, when you meet people from the potential employer you are likely to have an advantage if you genuinely want to work with them as your real enthusiasm will be picked up. If there were two candidates who meet the requirements, who would you give preference to? The one who isn't sure about the company, or the one who seems really keen?

By doing some background investigation you can build your enthusiasm and, as you might imagine, employers will view favourably the fact that you have taken the trouble to learn about them. Or of course you may decide from your research that it would be a mistake to take the application any further. Either way, you are a winner.

In the previous chapter you read about the general things that organisations are looking for. Any clues you can pick up in your research that help you to be more specific about *this* company's requirements will help you in two further ways. Firstly, you can assess yourself against those requirements and, secondly, you can focus your preparation for the selection event more closely.

Networking

One good way of finding out about an organisation is by using personal contacts. This may seem obvious, but not everyone thinks of other people they know who might have some experience of the company. Clearly, if you know people who already work there, they will be ideal to talk to - and more importantly to listen to. If you don't already know people who work there, maybe you know someone who knows someone . . . it's worth asking the people you do know if they have any contacts. They might be prepared to make an introduction, and if you offered lunch, coffee, a pint, this would help! They don't have to be current employees. Maybe they have worked there in the past, or been a customer, supplier or shareholder. This is often called "networking".

The term "networking" is used in this context to mean getting information from other people by tapping the contacts you already have, and by building further contacts. It is the same technique that serious job-hunters use to make it known that they are "on the market". Many people find that this helps them to learn about positions they would otherwise have missed, or that it gives them an entry point, an introduction, that helps them to find out information that is not usually available in the company's publications. It is also the way that many people keep their knowledge of the market fresh and up to date.

The term "networking" can also be seen in a negative light - in the same way as playing politics in an organisation can be viewed as manipulative. Don't be put off by this, but be aware that there is a fine line between being seen as curious and interested on the one hand, and being a nuisance on the other. If you only make contact with people to serve your own ends, they are likely to be less helpful to you than if it is a two-way process, where both parties feel that they have gained. The best and most effective networks are founded on mutual respect and maintained because the people involved get on well with each other and enjoy the discussions they have.

Your objective is to have conversations with people who can give you information about the organisation you are interested in. Your network might contain such people already. Alternatively, it might contain people who can introduce you to someone who can help you.

How to Get Started

Whether you know it or not, you already have a network. It may at this stage appear to be one that is not very useful, but it is surprising how quickly you can get from one contact to another. First of all, you can make a start by making an inventory of the people you know. But instead of doing this as a list, which can be limiting, try using a technique called "mind mapping" which is easier to add to. It helps you to put a large amount of information on a single sheet of paper. Start with an A4 sheet - but position it landscape (with the long edge at the top instead of the side). In the centre of your mind map you have the main theme - network. Then there will be strands running from this in all directions. Your strands might be:

- Family.
- Friends.
- Members of the clubs or societies you belong to.
- People you worked with in the past.
- Parents of your children's friends.

Each of these strands can have sub-strands - for instance "family" could divide into your own family and that of your spouse or partner; people you worked with in the past might sub-divide into the different jobs you have held.

When you start to put names on your map, you may be surprised at how many people you know! The beauty of a mind map is that you can keep adding to it without having to start all over again.

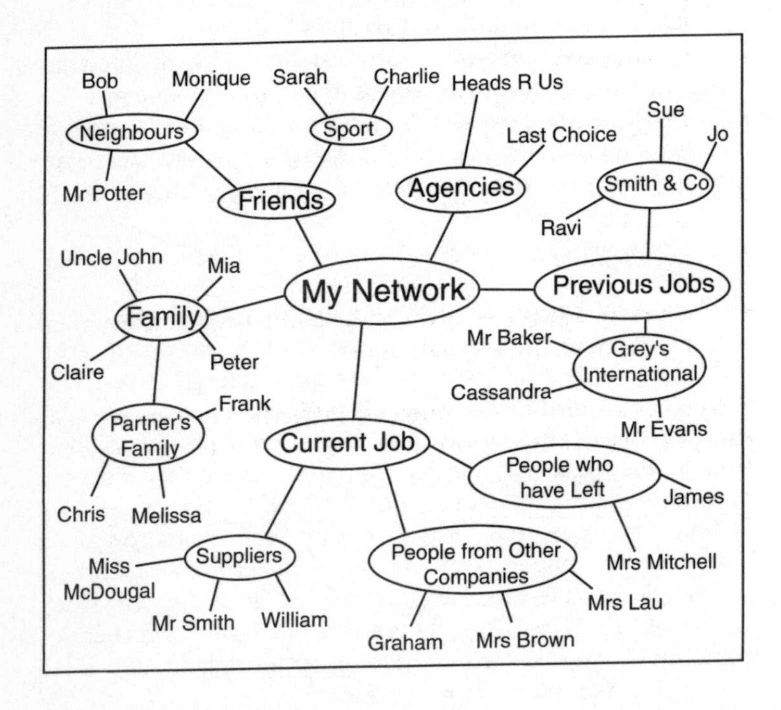

Fig. 9. Example mind map.

Every person on your mind map will have contacts of his or her own, so you can view each person as a starting point for another potential set of contacts. This is how you can use and develop your network.

Obviously, this does not often happen by chance. You need to let people know what you are interested in so that they can help you. Let's say the organisation you want to find out about deals in components for the motor industry. You might be lucky enough to find someone who works for them now, or who has worked for them in the past. However, they are not the only people who will have something to say about the company. You might find through your network:

- **Employees** – past or present.
- **Suppliers** – of goods or services.
- **Customers** – those who buy the company's goods to assemble into cars or use as spares to make repairs.
- **Consumers** – those who directly use the products and may have had cause to complain about them – good information here about how the organisation deals with the public.
- **Competitors** – people working for a rival company often have a view about their competitors.
- **Shareholders** – may track the company's performance and receive the annual report.

This gives an idea of the range of different perspectives you can get about any organisation by talking to people who have had contact with them.

"No, this is what they did after *I complained."*

Consumers who directly use the products and may have had cause to complain about them.

Some companies are part of a larger organisation – you might get information about the parent company. This will be of particular interest to you if you are thinking of a long-term career, and may want to pursue this in different subsidiary companies. It would be good to know, for instance, how common it is for people to move from one company to another, or what the parent company's main strategy is – are they likely to want to retain the company you are interested in or does it depart from their central interest?

Using your Network

Hopefully, your network will lead you to someone who knows about the company – ideally someone who works there. To help you get the most out of your discussion, you might want to make a list of questions that you would like answered. Open questions, i.e. those that encourage the other person to give you a lot of information, are going to be the most productive. "What's it like to work there?" is an example of an open question, and is likely to give you more information than "Is it a good place to work?" which could leave you with a yes/no response. Other questions you might pose to an employee are:

- How much involvement do you have in decisions?
- What do you most like about the place?
- What do you least like?
- Why do people generally leave?
- What's the attitude to training/personal development?
- How much support do you get?
- What sort of people get on well in the company?

Remember, your objective is to find out more about the company so that you can judge for yourself whether or not it's a place you would fit into and do well in. This is not a time to try to sell yourself or convince the other person – although making a good impression rather than a poor one can do no harm.

Why do people generally leave?

Other Sources of Information

Whilst people provide a great source of information, they are not always around when you want them, and in any case it is a good idea to use other sources to build up your picture of the organisation you are interested in.

Some of these sources may appear obvious to you - but they are included anyway as a reminder! There are two main categories:

- Information provided by the organisation.
- Information produced by a source outside the organisation, usually the media.

When you are looking at information about the organisation, you should ask yourself why it has been presented in that way. Why have they used those words or images? If the information is in company literature, it may tell you something about their values, how they want to appear and their aspirations. For example, if you look at an annual report and notice that there are personal statements and photographs of the senior management team, this may tell you that they want to be known and seen as individuals rather than as faceless officers of the company who are unapproachable. The tone of a news report may be over-sensational because it makes a better story!

If we start with sources that are provided by the organisation, these can be both direct - as with the company report and their product catalogue - or indirect - such as the advertisements about their products or their website. The latter are less direct because they have probably been produced by an intermediary like an advertising agency. Don't forget to have another look at the job advertisement if you responded to one. That too will give you clues about what the company thinks is important.

Company reports are often tedious to read, because there are regulations about how this information is presented. Many companies now produce a summary that is more palatable and, for your purposes, more useful. It is more likely to give information about how the company sees itself and where its future direction lies. Any marketing literature is likely to be useful in this way too. It is there to sell the company as well as the products and services, and will contain clues as to how the company wants to be seen. You might find terms such as:

- Increased globalisation - or, alternatively, Increased focus on key markets.
- Diversification - or Specialisation.
- Acquiring new businesses - or Divesting part of the portfolio.
- Controlling services - or Outsourcing non-core activity.
- Streamlining/Rationalising - or Expanding.
- Maximising shareholder value - or Steady, sustainable growth.

The depth you want to go to in exploring company information will depend on the nature of your role. However, you want to start building a picture that tells you about the competences the company is likely to require, the success criteria it is likely to set, and the values it expresses.

Then there are the stories about the company you will glean from other sources - trade and financial press, specific news items, sponsorship of events and community activities. You might think about what this tells you about the company's profile, how it communicates with the outside world, whether it is effective in managing its image and where it chooses to contribute to the community. Is it driven by altruism or the wish to use as many means as possible to market its products? You can get the information from:

- Libraries - large ones often can get hold of company information for you.
- Internet - this is likely to be your richest source, including accessing the company website and making on-line searches.
- Directly from the company - ask for literature.

Making Use of the Information

You will undoubtedly be able to gather more information than you need. Some kind of sifting and filtering will help to keep it manageable. Rather than wading through everything, it will be more efficient to scan through with some key headlines in mind. These should include specific questions you have about the company that will influence whether or not you want to work for it, and the areas mentioned in the last chapter.

Summary

This chapter has looked at ways of finding out about the company you have applied to. The potential value of your network has been stressed, and there are other sources of information that will help you.

When building up your picture of the company, try to distil out what you learn about the competences. See if you can produce three competences for each of the main headings: Business, Interpersonal and Individual, that you think the company will want to assess.

The following format may be helpful.

Competences	**1**	**2**	**3**
Business			
Interpersonal			
Individual			

Use what you know about the company to create a profile of the kind of person they want based on the seven signs of success. You may want to use this framework.

Themes	**Things I know the company wants**	**Things I think the company may want**
Track record		
Benchmarking		
Values		
Credibility		
Flexibility		
Holistic approach		
Receptiveness to learning		

Chapter 4:

The Selection Process

You've applied for a position and your application has convinced the company that you are someone they would like to find out more about. You have at least some of the things they are looking for in terms of your background, qualifications and experience. However, they will still have questions about you, and they hope to be able to answer these by putting you through the next stage in their selection procedure.

The kinds of selection exercises and activities you are likely to come across are covered in more detail later in this book. Of course, you are unlikely to be asked to participate in all of them when being considered for one position. This chapter helps you to make sure you know exactly what you are likely to face when you attend for assessment.

How Many Meetings?

Whether you are asked to attend on just one day or to be available for different exercises or meetings on different days will depend on a number of factors. The first sifting of candidates is done by inspecting the applications they have submitted, but even after this there will sometimes be a screening stage to produce a short list. Typically this will be an interview or "Assessment Centre", so your invitation might be for short-listing or final selection. Sometimes the short-listing is done by an agency, but the final decision will be taken by the company.

Another reason for having more than one meeting is that there are different managers who need to meet short-listed candidates, and they are not available on the same day. The person who is going to be your boss is likely to want to meet the final few candidates, but may not be prepared to spend time assessing a larger number. The more senior the position, the more likely it is that you will be asked to return and meet other people before a final decision is taken. As this can draw things out, you might want to know whether the event you attend is for short-listing, final selection or an intermediate part in the process.

Your Briefing

The information you receive will tell you where to attend and at what time. Some companies will automatically send a detailed briefing about the selection event, telling you who you will meet, what the selection process is and how long it is likely to last. If you don't get this, it is worth a phone call so that you can be prepared for the type of selection procedure. Before making the call, spend some time thinking about the questions you will ask so that you only have to call once. If you write them down leaving spaces, you can also jot the answers on the same sheet and thereby make sure you have covered all the queries you had.

The person who sent you the letter of invitation is likely to be your first port of call, unless of course the letter names someone else who can answer your queries. However, the invitation may have come from an administrator who does not know about the process in detail, in which case you will need to establish who can tell you more: "Who's the person I should speak to who can answer some questions about the selection process?"

Bear in mind that the people you speak to will have other work to do, and you will need to be sensitive to their pressures and demands. You could start by checking that they have the time to spend a few minutes talking to you: "I'm attending an Assessment Centre next week for the production supervisor job. I've got a few questions – is it convenient for you to talk to me just now?" – and, if not, ask when a better time would be: "When would be a good time for me to call back?"

Listen carefully to the answers and make sure you have understood them. A good technique is to summarise back: "So there'll be about five other candidates and we'll be asked to discuss something as a group."; "I'll have to make a presentation, but there's nothing you want me to do to prepare in advance."

Most selection events will include at least one interview. This could be with the person who will be your manager, to whom you will report, or someone else. Often a member of the personnel or human resources section will interview candidates, and in some organisations an outside consultant will be involved in some way to make an assessment. You might want to know who you will meet and who will interview you, because you will also be making a judgment about whether you want to join this organisation. It is important that you get on with the person who is going to be your boss or a colleague, however it is less important that you like the interviewer if it is someone you are unlikely to meet again – as is often the case with an outside consultant.

You may also want to know if you are being seen on your own, or if there will be other candidates there. It is not unheard of to meet other candidates that you already know, particularly if you are working in a field where there are limited opportunities. If you do not want it known generally that you are putting yourself forward for this position it could be embarrassing unless you are prepared for this possibility. Of course you wouldn't expect to know who the other candidates are, but you may prefer to know in advance that you will be meeting some.

Some of these questions may be ones that you are happy to have answered on the day, so be selective about how much information you ask for in advance. You don't want to be seen as too anxious!

"Fancy meeting you here, I thought you were at the dentist."

It is not unheard of to meet other candidates that you already know.

Assessment Centres

It is becoming more common for selection events to contain a number of different activities, and for the assessment of candidates to be made by more than one person. Such events are called "Assessment Centres". An Assessment Centre is not a place; neither is it a particular process. The term is a generic one for any event that allows candidates to be assessed over a number of different activities and by different assessors. The reason that this approach is growing is because it provides a more complete picture of candidates and has been shown to be more equitable.

An Assessment Centre Timetable

9.00	Candidates welcomed and briefed.
9.15	Presentation about the company.
9.30	Group exercise.
10.30	Coffee break.
10.45	Psychometric tests.
11.45	In-tray exercise.
12.45	Lunch – buffet with other members of the team.
1.30	Interviews and opportunity to see the company video.

Candidates free to go after their interview – interviews timetabled at 1.30, 2.15 and 3.00 pm.

Fig. 10. Assessment Centre timetable.

Interviews

Interviews alone have traditionally been notoriously unreliable as a way of making selection decisions. This is because in the past interviewers often lacked the skills needed to get the information they required to make good decisions; even those who were well trained could be influenced by their own prejudices and preconceptions. They might, for instance, have positive feelings towards someone who went to the same school as they did, or who was brought up in the same town. They might not like the idea of managing a person older than them or cleverer than them. These feelings are often subtle and difficult to eradicate.

These days interviews, and indeed other parts of the selection event, are more likely to be structured around areas that are important for success in the job. This partly results from better training in the techniques of interviewing and how to make objective selection decisions, and partly from laws to protect some groups from unfair discrimination. Employers have to be able to justify their decisions by referring to the evidence they collect through the selection event. For instance, it is not acceptable to reject a candidate because she is female, but it is quite reasonable to reject someone because the job involves planning one's own time and the interview evidence was that the candidate depended on other people to organise her.

An interview may be the selection device, or it may form part of a larger Assessment Centre.

Questions you might want to ask about the Interview:

- Who will be conducting the interview?
- Is this the person to whom you would report if appointed?
- Will there be just the one interviewer, or a panel?
- If other people are there, what are their roles?
- How long is the interview likely to last?
- Will there be an opportunity for you to ask questions?

Group Exercises

Where the job involves working with other people - and of course most jobs do, whether this is with colleagues, clients, customers or project teams - there will often be a group discussion exercise. Group exercises allow the assessors to see how you interact with other people to reach a decision or solve a problem. Sometimes the task will be to achieve a consensus, or you may be asked to take a certain position and try to get others in the group to agree with you. It may not be clear whether there is a right answer or not - often the issue you are asked to discuss has different possible solutions. However, by watching and listening, the assessors will be able to collect information about how you contribute in a group, and also the quality of your ideas. Generally there will be no advance preparation that you can do before you arrive on the day.

Questions you might want to ask about a Group Exercise:

- How many will be in the group?
- Will the exercise require any specialist knowledge?

In-tray Exercises

Sometimes you will be asked to work on a simulation of the kinds of tasks you would be required to undertake if appointed. This is sometimes called an "in-tray" exercise because it uses the kinds of items a job-holder might have in his or her in-tray. Typically you would work on this on your own, and other candidates might be working on the same exercise alongside you.

This is sometimes called an in-tray exercise.

Questions you might want to ask about an In-tray Exercise:

- Does the exercise require specialist knowledge?
- What form of response is required – e.g. written or keyboard?

Presentations

Another common Assessment Centre exercise is a presentation. This is often included when the job involves making presentations, training other people or selling. You might also be asked to make a presentation if the role could be developed in different ways, to give you an opportunity of explaining how you would take it forward. Sometimes the presentation is one which you will be asked to prepare on the day, usually using just a flipchart and with limited time to put it all together.

If you are asked to prepare a presentation in advance, you will need to make sure you know what type of presentation is expected and how long it should last. You may be accustomed to presenting from an overhead projector, in which case you would want to check that one will be available. If you want to use slides, you will need to know if they have a projector, how it operates and whether the room can be easily darkened. Some people are most comfortable presenting from a pc, in which case you need to ensure that you can either take all the equipment with you, or that theirs is compatible with yours. You will want to know how many people are likely to be in your audience – even if only so that you can prepare an adequate number of handouts in the event of a power failure!

There is more about preparing for presentations in Chapter 7 along with information about other Assessment Centre exercises you might come across.

Questions you might want to ask about Presentations:

- To whom will I be presenting?
- How long should the presentation last?
- What equipment is available?

Tests

Most Assessment Centres will include some kind of testing. There are many different types of test that can be used, some which tap into specific skills needed to do the job (such as driving, typing, using a spreadsheet) and others which look at more generic abilities which relate to successful performance (such as numerical or verbal ability). These are quantitative, in that the result of the test is a single score that shows how well you performed. Then there are more qualitative tests which are more about how you approach things. These might look at your personality, values or attitudes. Typically the results of these would be represented as a profile indicating tendencies and preferences.

Psychometric tests - literally "mind measuring" - are those designed to assess generic abilities (quantitative) or personality characteristics (qualitative) by comparing your performance or pattern of responses to that of a reference group. The reference group might be "graduates", or "insurance sales reps" or "general population". Tests of more specific job skills are more likely to measure your performance against a standard required for the job. They are not psychometric, as they are not measuring abilities or characteristics that we assume everyone has, albeit with individual differences. Instead, they test how well you have learnt to do something and whether you have achieved the standard of performance required to do the job.

More imaginative employers who intend training you for a particular job will include a mini-training session as part of the assessment, to see how easily you pick up the required skills. Whilst this is a very reliable and effective way of making selection decisions, there is a limited range of jobs for which this is feasible.

Questions you might want to ask about Testing:

- Will there be testing involved in the assessment?
- What form of tests will be used?
- How long do the tests last?
- If numerical ability is tested, will calculators be used? Will the test be arithmetic or to do with analysis of numerical data?

- If verbal ability is tested, what form of test is used – vocabulary or reasoning based on verbal information?
- What part do the tests play in the assessment procedure?

A General Note about Assessment Centres

A word of warning: Assessment Centres often involve some time when you are not occupied. There will usually be more candidates than assessors, and if there are individual interviews or presentations you will have to wait your turn. You will be expected to be available, so it is usually not possible to arrange to do anything else. Of course, there might be a supply of newspapers and company information for you to read, but you might want to take a book just in case! Also, don't assume that you can escape at lunchtime to go to some other appointment. Arrangements may have been made for you to meet other employees or have a guided tour, and it would not look good if you disappeared.

Summary

The intention in this chapter has been to make sure you know what to expect when you attend the selection event, so that you can do some preparation and turn up feeling more confident. If you do need to speak to someone to find out more about the event, spend a few minutes beforehand writing down what you already know from the information sent to you, and then the questions you want to ask.

Here is a Checklist to help you:

- Start time and place.
- Finish time.
- Who I will meet.
- Interview only or Assessment Centre.
- Interview - single interviewer or panel.
- What other exercises - group, individual?
- Equipment available (if preparing a presentation).
- Tests - specific skill, psychometric.
- Final stage or next hurdle.

Chapter 5:

Psychological Tests – Personality

About Personality Tests

The word "test" conjures up something that you can either pass or fail, or do well at or poorly at. However, personality tests are a bit different. Generally speaking, there is no way to fail a personality test. Depending on how it is being used in the selection process - and more about that later in this chapter - it is also not usually a question of doing well or doing poorly. In that respect, the word "test" is not a good description of the sort of measurement being used when you are asked to complete a questionnaire about your personality. In effect, by filling in your responses you are describing yourself in a particular way, and that way is to do with the dimensions and characteristics measured by the test.

When your responses are scored up, they will reveal a profile of your personality. If you have responded honestly, you would probably recognise the profile as being a good description of the sort of person you are - albeit a partial one as any test will only look at some aspects of your personal style. So, for instance, if you regard yourself as a very energetic and motivated person, and the test includes a measure of drive, the profile should include that attribute. However, you might also consider yourself to be generous, but unless this quality is one of those included, this would not appear on your profile.

Many people are surprised at how accurate these tests appear to be, but when you consider that the profile is only telling you what you have already revealed by your responses, this is really not so surprising! The clever part comes from the basis on which these tests are constructed, and explains why some tests are better than others at predicting how people will behave.

The best tests look at dimensions or characteristics that underlie a lot of our behaviour, such as how adventurous or outgoing people are. A large group of people would be asked the same set of questions, and then other evidence would be gathered about, for instance, how adventurous they are. A very timid person who never takes risks and has to be encouraged to try anything new will respond to the questions differently from someone who is bored by routine, always wants to have a go at new experiences and goes out of her way to try new things. These are extremes of the dimension. Most people are not extreme, but fall somewhere between the two so that although we use similar words to describe people sharing a characteristic, this does not mean that they are exactly the same.

An analogy might be with eye colour. Superficially, we can say that many people have brown eyes. However, when we look at a lot of people with brown eyes we notice that some are darker brown than others, and that in fact there is a range between almost yellow and nearly black. We can then start to see how many people have very yellowish eyes versus mid-brown versus nearly black eyes. Of course, eye colour is not something that should be of importance to many employers, and in any case is not a feature of your personality. What we usually find when we look at personality characteristics is that relatively few people are well described by the extremes, and many more fall into the central area of the dimension.

Not all characteristics show this distribution. In fact, if we stick with the eye colour analogy, we know that whilst there may be a lot of variation *within* a colour, there are also distinctly different colours – some people don't have brown eyes, so we need another dimension to describe, for example how deeply purply blue they are at one end, and pale powder blue at the other.

With some personality characteristics, there is a debate as to whether they are accurately described as one dimension or two distinct ones. An example of this is introversion–extroversion. A popular personality instrument is the Myers Briggs Type Indicator - the MBTI. This questionnaire is based on the idea that there are four distinct areas where people differ, one of these being introversion–extroversion. Whereas most measures would say that this is a single dimension, the MBTI shows it as a bi-polar characteristic - a bit like brown-eyed and blue-eyed, where most people have *either* brown *or* blue eyes - not both. Another analogy would be left-handed or right-handed. This is a closer analogy for a personality characteristic, because we can see that there is a difference between how a left-handed and right-handed person will perform the same task - in other words a link between being right-handed and a person's behaviour. However we can also recognise different degrees of right-handedness or left-handedness. So while all left-handed people share some similarities, there are also differences between left-handed people relating to how strongly they prefer using their left hand. In this way, we can build up two distinct distributions. (Fig. 11 shows the difference between conceptualising introversion-extroversion as a single or bi-polar characteristic.)

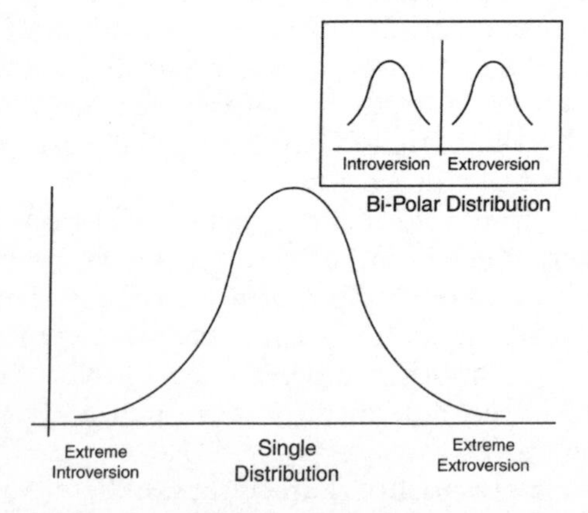

Fig. 11. Two different ways of conceptualising introversion-extroversion.

The MBTI is more often used to help people gain self-insight and to understand the behaviour of their colleagues. You are less likely to come across it as a selection tool.

There are many different personality questionnaires. Some are very long and take up to an hour to complete, whilst others may only take a few minutes. Some are designed to be clearly related to the working environment, while others are more general and the questions may seem to be completely unrelated to work.

"It's a really long questionnaire. If they stick with it, we say they are tenacious."

Some personality questionnaires are very long and take up to an hour to complete.

What do we mean by "Personality"?

We all describe ourselves by reference to other people we know. So if you think you are very energetic, it is likely that you know a lot of people who are less energetic than you are and only a few – if any – who are more so. Personality tests make the same kind of judgment, comparing you to a large group of people and saying whether you are, for instance, more or less adventurous than most other people.

There has been a lot of research into the kinds of characteristics that make good predictions about how people behave more generally. This is based on the idea that we all have "traits" that are consistent across many different kinds of situations, and that endure throughout our lives. So if you were very energetic as a youngster, you are likely to remain that way in adult life. If you are keen to try new things in your leisure time, you are likely to enjoy variety at work. If you related to people in a cool way in your last job, you're likely to repeat this in the next one. Of course, there will be a lot of things about you that are consistent, but less easy to measure – so you won't be asked any questions about your charisma!

Some personality characteristics are clearly related to our genetic make-up. Even if we don't yet know exactly how personality is inherited, we have enough evidence from our knowledge of similarities within families even where the different family members have been raised separately to know that at least some things are with us from the very start. However, with the same starting point, we can go off in very different directions. Our early experiences, particularly in terms of the kind of behaviour that was rewarded and approved of as opposed to punished or discouraged, will be influential in shaping our adult persona.

After many years of investigation into the factors that make up someone's personality, it is now widely accepted that there are five major themes that are central to the enduring features of a person's character. They are expressed as dimensions, and individuals differ in terms of where they sit along each dimension. Leaving aside the MBTI, which is based on a different model of the components of personality, most questionnaires cover some or all of these five major dimensions, which are:

1. Introversion–extroversion. This relates to your orientation to the world, whether it is largely internally or externally focused. People who are more introvert by nature are often more comfortable in small groups or on their own rather than with lots of other people. They are likely to have within their leisure interests at least some pursuits that are solitary, such as reading or running. When expressing views, they will usually think before they speak. Extroverts are often stimulated by things in the outside world – other people and activities. They may be more active and sociable, and less inclined to reflect deeply on their own characteristics.

2. Emotionally calm–emotionally energetic. This dimension relates to your response to events, either as they happen or in anticipation. Those at the calm end of the dimension are less likely to find that many things arouse strong feelings, whereas at the energetic end they might be more anxious or driven. Emotional energy can be both a positive and a negative feature. When it is directed positively it motivates people to work hard, perhaps to make sure that they don't fail. Another positive side is that by expressing emotions people communicate the strength of their commitment and belief. However, sometimes anxiety about failure can stop people from doing things and make them risk-averse. The calm end can be seen as balanced and professional, or alternatively cool and remote.

3. Imaginative–conservative. Some people are highly creative by nature – although creativity is a skill as well as a personality characteristic. At the imaginative side, people find it easy to see possibilities and different angles to problems, although they might not always be realistic. The conservative end of the dimension is characterised by a preference for tried and tested methods, valuing experience and being "down to earth".

4. Conscientious–easygoing. This relates to the degree of self-discipline and sense of responsibility that people feel in general terms. Those who are very conscientious are likely to prefer being organised and reliable, but they might also be rigid about following rules and see the world in a somewhat black and white way. At the more easygoing end of the dimension we find people who might be more flexible and expedient, but who might also be careless.

5. Co-operative–competitive. People differ in the extent to which they feel bound to resolve conflict or avoid it, versus being prepared to stick to their guns and fight their corner. Those at the co-operative end of the spectrum generally prefer harmonious relationships and will work hard to accommodate other people. They might compromise to reach consensus and go along with what other people want. At the competitive end, people are more likely to confront and challenge, and might push harder to get their own way.

From this set of personality dimensions, it is possible to make some predictions about the kinds of work individuals will naturally gravitate to, but of course this is only part of the picture.

Other Factors that Affect how People Behave and Make Choices

The direction of people's intellectual strengths, their values and beliefs and the impact of their experience will also play a major part in determining where they find themselves most satisfyingly employed. The effect of motivation cannot be over-stated too. People who are determined to succeed in a particular area can often overcome the possible limitations that their personality or natural talents might appear to contain.

Experience may not change someone's personality, any more than it changes whether you are right-handed or left-handed, but it can have a significant effect on your attitude to work and life in general. Many people find that a major life experience, such as the death of a loved one, a painful divorce or the birth of their first child, changes the way they view the world. The loss of a valued relationship

The effect of motivation cannot be over-stated.

can make people who are highly conscientious see things in perspective and become more relaxed and balanced in their outlook. The responsibilities of parenthood sometimes make someone more reliable and conscious of security.

Then there is the more gradual learning that takes place as we gain more life experience and meet different kinds of people. Some people are more receptive to this kind of learning, and tend to become more tolerant of others, more likely to value others' opinions and different strengths and more willing to expose themselves to new situations and environments. Those who are less affected by their life experience might find that they protect themselves against change and retreat more into their "comfort zone".

Clearly, questionnaires are inadequate to cover the full range of individual difference or to provide a complete picture of any individual. In most cases an organisation will select the characteristics that are most important to it either in terms of being successful in the job or being a valuable addition to an existing team.

Where the position requires specific leadership capabilities and the environment is likely to be changing, and especially where the role is key to the success of the organisation, a more in-depth individual analysis might be employed. This might be a more personal and individual assessment, not necessarily based solely on particular personality characteristics. The level of expertise required to undertake such an analysis usually means that you would be asked to meet an external consultant for a number of hours. This kind of assessment is covered in more detail in Chapter 9.

The Use of Personality Tests

Personality tests used as part of a selection procedure should contain characteristics that are relevant to the job you are applying for. However, it takes a lot of research to put together a good personality test. In the ideal world one might wish to have many different tests representing the full spectrum of occupations and work environments, but in reality the test you are asked to complete is likely to be a more general one that has already been researched and can be used as an indicator in a variety of situations.

Most personality questionnaires ask you to make a choice - either to select a statement that fits you best, to select from a range of responses to a statement, or to say whether you agree or disagree with a statement. Sometimes you are given the option of saying you neither agree nor disagree, although where this is the case you are generally guided to choose this option as infrequently as possible. In other words, you are urged to fall on one side or the other.

Example 1

State which of the following best describes you:

I learn a lot by reading books.
I have to do something myself before I have learnt it.
I'd rather watch someone else before I try something new.

In that example you might think that all the statements are true for you, but you have to choose which is the best description – the one which is true more often, or which you are most committed to.

Example 2

Possible responses:
Always.
Usually.
Sometimes.
Rarely.
Never.

Which response would you give for the following statements?

When I go on holiday I like to go somewhere I've never been before.

Before I go to the supermarket I make a list of the things I want to buy.

If someone I know slightly invites me to a party, I accept.

Here you were given five possible responses and you had to select which was the response that represents what you would do. You might want to say that it depends on some other factor, but of course the questionnaire doesn't give you that opportunity. So you need to think about what would be true for you in most situations.

Example 3

For each statement tick:

(a) If you agree.
(b) If you neither agree nor disagree.
(c) If you disagree.

Tick only one. Try to avoid the (b) option if you can.

I enjoy going out with a lot of people.
When I see sad films I often feel like crying.
I easily get bored when I'm on my own.
Rules should never be broken.
I care what other people think of me.

When you are asked to make a choice given statements like these it is sometimes difficult to decide what to say. The easy option is to keep going for the middle ground – but you are asked not to do that! The frustrating thing about this kind of questionnaire is that you probably want to put in caveats and moderators. "I care about what other people think of me – but only if they are people I like/respect/fear."

Unfortunately, you are not given the opportunity to explain why you responded to a particular question in the way you did. You need to choose one response that is true for you most of the time.

In reality, when scoring the test to create your profile, the individual questions are not looked at. The scoring technique is to count the number of responses of a particular type for each group of questions – and the group of questions is likely to be scattered within the test. So, for instance, the scorer may count how many (a) responses there are to questions 1, 7, 9, 14, 15, 18, etc. to see how adventurous you are relative to most other people, or how many (c) responses to a different group of questions to see how much you like working on your own.

Describing your Own Personality

You might want to take some time to reflect on your personality in terms of some of the measurable and consistent traits that have been described in this chapter. Be careful not to think of one side of the scale as being better than the other. Whether a characteristic is good or bad often depends on the situation and also how it relates to other characteristics. Also, try to avoid thinking about a specific occasion. The ability to behave in a certain way is not the issue. We can all act "out of character" or make an effort to do things that don't come naturally to us, but these incidents don't reflect our true personality. Instead, think about how you would behave given a truly free choice, and also how the people who know you best might describe you. As you read through the following, you are bound to find some features that you agree with in the description of both ends of the dimension. However, one might appear to be more like you than the other.

Where would you put yourself on the Introversion/Extroversion Dimension?

At the extrovert end we have people who seek out other people, who are stimulated by activity in the outside world, who are socially outgoing. They might do things impulsively and enjoy adventure and variety. In general, they would feel comfortable when amongst a large group of people. They might feel energised by talking to others whilst they hate spending prolonged time alone. Often they might appear to change their minds because they have talked about their ideas before being certain of what they think. Others would see them as loud, expressive, spontaneous, with a liking for being amongst people.

At the introvert end we have people who prefer to spend time away from other people, who are stimulated by thoughts, reflections and ideas and are socially reserved. They might think things through before acting and therefore appear more consistent in their views. It is likely that they feel most comfortable with just one or two other people, with small rather than large groups. They might be fatigued by interacting with a lot of people and need time alone to recharge their batteries. Others would see them as quiet, reflective, contemplative with a preference for being on their own.

Where would you put yourself on this dimension? It is quite possible to be a sociable and adventurous introvert, just as it is possible to be a quiet and cautious extrovert. This is because there are many factors that contribute to the characteristic, and indeed gives an indication of why there is so much difference between individuals. However, most people would be able to say where, on balance, they lie on the dimension.

Where would you put yourself on the Emotionally Calm/Energetic Scale?

People who are emotionally calm might find that it takes a lot to upset them and they seldom feel strong emotions. Their tolerance of frustration might be high and they can generally keep things in perspective. They would be seen by others as balanced, steady, objective and emotionally restrained. When they think about the future it is likely to be in a realistic way, neither overly optimistic or pessimistic.

The emotionally energetic are likely to show a greater level of anxiety. They might be nervous of trying new things, but feel driven to try them anyway. Or their anxieties might be so great that they choose not to take the risk. They would be seen as having a sense of urgency, to get emotional more easily and to be less consistent in their behaviour.

How do you see yourself here? Does it take a lot to arouse

your emotions, to get you excited or passionate about something or to upset you or make you angry? Or do you have a high "resting" level of emotion, whether or not you always show it?

Where would you put yourself on the Imaginative/Conservative Dimension?

At the imaginative end people are likely to enjoy generating new ideas and ways of doing things. They like to try something different. They will often look at situations from different, maybe surprising, perspectives and be flexible. Other people would see them as open-minded, intuitive, maybe creative, and at times so attracted by change that they run the risk of "throwing out the baby with the bathwater".

Those who are conservative rely on past experience and put their trust in tried and tested methods. They might not be resistant to change, but would be characterised by needing to be convinced that it was required. They know the value of using traditional approaches and are likely to be more suspicious of "flavour of the month" ideas. They want to know the facts rather than being swayed by the possibilities. Other people might see them as stubborn if they disagree with them, or well-grounded if they agree!

Can you see where you lie on this dimension? Would your slogan be "If it ain't broke, don't fix it"? Or perhaps, at the other end of the scale, you find it dull when things carry on much the same as before.

Where would you put yourself on the Conscientious/Easygoing Dimension?

Conscientious people like to know the rules, and they are reliable in sticking to them. They have a strong sense of responsibility and hate to let other people down. They can err by being rigidly attached to rules, so that they come across at times as inflexible when situations are ambiguous

. . . put their trust in tried and tested methods.

and there are no guidelines. They usually have a definite sense of what is right and wrong, and other people would see them as principled, conforming and self-disciplined.

Easygoing people are relaxed about rules and procedures. They are likely to decide on a course of action depending on the circumstances and what seems best at the time rather than worrying about whether it is in line with what is acceptable. They might be egalitarian and ignore convention regarding hierarchical relationships. Other people would see them as expedient, unconventional - even eccentric at the extreme - and flexible.

How would you describe yourself in these terms? Are rules there to be broken or would you feel a sense of responsibility for following them even if you didn't fully agree with them?

Where would you put yourself on the Co-operative/Competitive Dimension?

At the co-operative end we see people who seek consensus or at least reassurance before doing something, who will compromise and accommodate other people's wishes. They might respect other people for making decisions and sometimes prefer this to making unpopular decisions themselves. They might feel that it was important to have people around to help them think things through, sharing responsibility and moving forward as a team. Others would see them as involving other people, being helpful and sensitive to others' needs.

At the competitive end we might have those who make their mind up about what they're going to do before talking it through with anyone else. They might prefer to solve their own problems and might even consider it a weakness to involve anyone else. They are likely to be decisive and prepared to push their decisions even when these are unpopular. Other people would see them as self-reliant, perhaps controlling and able to take charge, and liking autonomy.

Which end of the dimension best describes you? Do you involve other people because you want to get a sense of shared ownership and responsibility, or do you do it only when there is a clear and tangible benefit in terms of the result? Are you more likely to confront differences of opinion and argue your corner, or will you usually try to avoid conflict and either compromise or back down?

Other Characteristics an Employer might Assess

The five main themes contain many different factors that tend to cluster together. However, an employer might be particularly interested in specific factors rather than the big package. You will often get an indication of what factors are important from the wording in the advertisement or the job description. Any words that seem to describe the type of person rather than the skill will be clues. Some examples are:

1. Independent – possibly relating to working without close supervision.

2. Confident – maybe to sell ideas or products with credibility.
3. Friendly – to fit in well with the existing team.
4. Resilient – able to work in stressful environments.
5. Reliable – dependable and trustworthy.
6. Creative – perhaps to come up with new ideas.
7. Thorough – detail-conscious and diligent.
8. Tough – prepared to stand your ground and make difficult decisions.
9. Flexible – able to adapt to different people and circumstances.
10. Sociable – possibly because building relationships is important.

Remember the caution about thinking one side of the scale was better than the other? Let's take the example of "independent". We all start life being completely dependent babies, and become more independent as we grow and learn. Our tendency to judge independence as being preferable may date back to our childhood, where we were encouraged to do more things for ourselves. However, the population you will be compared with won't contain children. It will be a sample of adults who have developed various levels of independence.

It is possible to be too independent to be comfortable in certain jobs; for instance if your success depends on following rules, and safety demands that you get a colleague to check what you have done, you could easily be frustrated if you were highly independent. You might quickly start to cut corners and perhaps compromise safety.

The important thing is to see the characteristic in context. Similarly with confidence. Whilst confidence is generally a good thing, a bit of anxiety is good for survival. Anxiety can make us work hard to be well-prepared; it can lead us to looking realistically for the dangers and pitfalls. We might appreciate some anxiety in an engineer designing a bridge that would carry us over a ravine, or in a factory worker making parachutes! Drive and ambition are often fuelled by a bit of anxiety.

Why does an Employer want to know about your Personality?

This is not a straightforward question to answer. When we think of specific jobs or roles it is easier to see why particular characteristics can help people to be successful – or can get in the way of their doing a good job. For instance, if the job was concerned with health and safety regulations, it is pretty obvious that you want to employ someone who is conscientious rather than easygoing about rules. There will be other areas where legal requirements and compliance to regulations are important and cannot be compromised. In these areas being both conscientious and competitive might be preferred.

What about an internal audit or training role? There might still be an argument for giving preference to candidates who were more conscientious than easygoing, but you might want them also to be more co-operative than competitive because the success of the organisation depends on reaching a solution that other people can work with.

If the position is in the purchasing department, and tough negotiation is called for, a more competitive style might be thought likely to be more successful than a co-operative one. However, increasingly there are partnerships with suppliers that require a more collaborative approach so that the supplying company can deliver the required quality of product at the agreed price. Being imaginative and flexible might therefore also be called for.

A personality profile from a questionnaire should never be used on its own to make a decision. In some cases, the selectors will be trying to get a more complete picture of the type of person you are, by adding the information from questionnaires to that they have gathered by other means, such as interview and observation of how you responded in a group exercise. It will help them to test their hypotheses, so that if your questionnaire profile matches the picture they have gained from other sources they can have more confidence in their judgment. Equally, if they have questions or concerns about how you would deal with different situations, the questionnaire profile might give them information that allows them to make sensible predictions.

In some cases they will have an idea of how a successful person behaves, and will use the questionnaire as a way of deciding whether or not you are likely to behave in a similar way. Some organisations will have a database of the profiles of people who have already been successful, and will look to see if your profile is similar. This is a probabilistic model – in effect they are saying that since people of this type have been successful in the past, there is a good chance that someone similar will be successful in the future. Whilst this has some appeal, it also has shortcomings, as it denies opportunities to people who could have been successful, but have a different style.

Of course, this model also falls short where the job is a new one, or where the requirements have changed over time, or where there is no database to cover the kind of role. In this situation they might be more interested to see if you have the kind of characteristics they believe will contribute to success, or be on the lookout for characteristics that would suggest you are unlikely to be a good fit for the role.

Other possibilities are that the employer already knows the profiles of the rest of the team you would be joining, and would prefer to employ someone with a different style.

Enlightened employers will look at the questionnaire profile as a way of identifying what help you might need to make you as successful as you can be. They will use your responses as a way of answering the question: "If we were to appoint you, what help or development would you need?" In terms of the decision-making, they might then reject candidates whose needs are beyond what they can supply, but take someone they believe they can help to be successful.

Your Approach to Personality Questionnaires

Whatever the rationale is for using personality questionnaires, you should be honest in your responses. If you are not, you run the danger of showing an inconsistent picture during the selection event because the profile on paper is markedly different from the person seen during other exercises. This can be off-putting to those making the selection decision and, even if they believe you have the capability to do the job, they may doubt your integrity. Even if you avoid this, and somehow manage to get the job, you may find that you have been selected for something that does not suit you – you might end up being unsuccessful or unhappy. It is easier to present what you think is a favourable front over the short time you are being assessed than it is during the long time you are in a job!

By being honest, you will be more confident that your employers know what they are getting when they offer you the job. They have selected you knowing as much about you as they can, and that includes the warts and all. When they know what weaknesses and limitations you have, it is more likely that they will be prepared to support and help you to overcome them. Used professionally, personality information can help an employer to help you in the way that you actually need, and there can be a win-win result.

After the Event – Feedback

Whether or not you were successful, it is a good idea to try to get feedback. Some organisations will offer this routinely, although of course they are unlikely to be able to give you a lot of time for this if you are not appointed. However, any information they can give you will be useful when you are considering what you do next – for instance, should you be thinking about different kinds of working environments that suit your personal style better? If there are apparent reasons for your rejection that you think you can address, are there things you can do to explain this at your next interview? Are there things about yourself that you need to re-assess so that you can be more effective generally?

Here are some examples of how feedback helped people:

"I was really disappointed not to get the job, but there was someone in their personnel department who spent a few minutes on the phone telling me why I wasn't chosen. She explained that they were looking for a team-player, and that the impression they had formed of me was that I was too independent. When I thought about it afterwards I had to admit that it was probably true. I often think I know best and had never really given much thought to how I could help other people do their jobs better. Even when I was on the school hockey team, I used to get angry with other players who made mistakes – when of course the best result was achieved if we were all supporting each other. The more I thought about it, the more examples I could come up with of times when I could have done more to help others get to a better result."

"In my company the next step for me is promotion into a management position. When a job came up I applied and was asked to attend an Assessment Centre. I didn't get the job, but the feedback has made me think more about what I want to do. At first it was very frustrating, because they told me how good I was at my current job – so I thought I deserved the promotion. But it also made me realise that being promoted would have meant doing something different, something I was less comfortable with. My personality profile confirmed that I was happy working largely on my own, being an expert in a relatively narrow field. I felt really stuck and was quite depressed for a while. Then I asked myself if I really wanted to do something different, or if I'd be happier doing more or less the same thing in a bigger company, where there were more opportunities to progress without becoming a manager. I haven't decided yet, but it's given me a different set of questions to ask myself. Previously I'd just been looking at promotion as being the important thing."

"A friend suggested I phone and ask for some feedback when I was turned down for a job. The manager who talked to me was very blunt with me, which I appreciated – although

not at the time! He told me I hadn't sold myself well. They thought I could probably do the job, but they had other applicants who gave them more confidence. He made some comment about my personality test, which suggested I was quite reserved and not very sociable, and the two things clicked into place for me. It made me more determined to do a better job at explaining what I could do next time, but it also made me think that I could do with some help in becoming more assertive generally."

Mini-tests

Here are three mini-personality tests for you to complete. They are not "proper" tests, but will give you an idea of the kinds of questions you might be faced with. At the end of this section is an explanation of the characteristics covered by each mini-test.

Mini-test A

Choose one of the following options to respond to each statement:

(a) Agree completely.
(b) Neither agree nor disagree.
(c) Disagree.

1. I often drive fast – I really enjoy it.
2. Older people often have valuable experience that the young could learn from.
3. Physical activity makes me feel great.
4. Children need to be disciplined.
5. I get impatient when people don't understand me.
6. Violent films should be subject to greater control.
7. It's often the case that I leave things to the last minute.
8. Many medicines are dangerous and need tighter restrictions.
9. Surprises make me feel uncomfortable.
10. People should stand up for their principles.

Mini-test B

Put a letter against each of the following statements.

(a) If this is true most of the time.
(b) If this is true sometimes.
(c) If this is seldom true.

1. I enjoy lively parties.
2. People think of me as popular.
3. After a busy day I just want to curl up in front of the television.
4. I can let the phone ring and not answer it.
5. If a friend invites me to something, I go.
6. I like to do things spontaneously.
7. My parents would tell you I was a shy child.
8. I think before I speak.
9. If I want to find something out I ask someone.

Mini-test C

Decide whether each of the following statements is true or false for you. You must make a choice one way or the other.

1. If someone comes to the door to read the meter, I check their identification before letting them in.
2. When someone asks me to lend them money, I usually do it.
3. You should avoid giving out your credit card number over the phone.
4. I rely on other people to do what they say they'll do.
5. You never know if beggars are really in need of help.
6. I've been let down by other people.
7. It's best to remind people when you have an appointment to meet them.
8. My friends would say I trust people too easily.

Mini-test A looked at two different personality characteristics. One was to do with how emotional you are – the odd numbered questions related to those. The other – the even numbered questions – was about how much you feel the need to control other people for their own good. In this case, only the (a) responses would have been counted.

Mini-test B looked at the introversion–extroversion dimension. Some of the questions (the first pair, third pair and last item) refer to typical extrovert behaviour, and the others to typical introvert preferences. Your responses would show whether you are predominantly an extrovert or introvert person.

Mini-test C is about how trusting as opposed to suspicious you are. The odd numbered statements would be more likely to be true for people at the suspicious end of the dimension, and the even numbered statements would be more likely to be false. The opposite would be the case with someone at the trusting end of the dimension.

Summary

This chapter has shown you what personality tests are, and why they are often used as part of a selection procedure. They are not the sorts of tests that you can pass or fail, but they can be useful in building up a picture of the kind of person you are. For them to help both the selectors and yourself you need to be honest in your responses. Preparation is not necessary, but you might want to familiarise yourself with possible kinds of questionnaires - and you have had a few examples of these - so that you are not nervous.

Gaining insight into your personality is valuable both in thinking about the kind of working environment that suits you, and in addressing the characteristics that might make you less attractive to an employer. You are therefore encouraged to get feedback whenever possible, whether or not you have been successful in your application.

Chapter 6:

Psychological Tests – Ability

The previous chapter dealt with measures of personality where there are no correct answers. This chapter looks at a different group of tests – the ones that really do have right and wrong answers. They are the kinds of tests that comprise problems for you to solve, and each problem has only one answer that is acceptable.

Ability tests are typically used to see if you have some very specific skills, or sometimes the underlying capability to acquire the skills needed to do the job. In other words, they are looking at how well you can perform certain tasks or solve a particular kind of problem. Ability and personality tests are both examples of "psychometric" tests. The word psychometric comes from the Greek words to do with "mind" and "measurement". This means that these tests relate to some mental process. In the case of ability tests, this is usually to do with how good you are at solving particular types of problems, or how quickly you process information. The tasks are therefore mental rather than physical. As with physical skills, some people are better than others at performing them. Even with a lot of practice there will always be some people who find it easier to achieve high performance than others. Individuals will eventually reach a point where they cannot get any better!

What is an Ability Test?

Some specific skills are easy to measure – for instance, if you were to be a keyboard operator or typist, the best way to measure how good you are would be to ask you to use a keyboard to perform a sample of the tasks typical of the general day-to-day work. Tests could be set up to compare your performance with that of other people – either those who are already competent or those with whom you are competing for the job. To be absolutely fair, the test would have to be the same for everyone.

Psychometric tests of mental abilities follow the same rule – they are constructed in such a way that they can be administered in the same way for everyone. They will compare your performance on the test with that of other people, so although there is always a right answer for each problem you are asked to tackle, it does not follow that you have to get everything right to be able to do the job. Using our typist as an analogy, we would regard candidates as very skilled if they made no more errors than those who were already excellent at doing the job.

All ability tests will have been constructed so that your performance can be compared with that of other people – a group who have previously taken the same test. The test will have been tried out with different groups of people, for instance, graduates or managers, and a relevant group chosen as a comparison group for you and the other candidates. Each group will show a distribution of results that indicates how well most people do when they complete the test. When tests are being constructed, they will be modified until the distribution – numbers of people who obtain different scores – forms the pattern of a bell-shaped curve. If the test is too easy, most people would get most of it correct so it would not be useful to identify high performers – even poor performers might get high scores. If it is too hard, even top performers would get a low score, and as it might be possible to get a few right by chance this does not help in making selection decisions.

The bell-shaped curve bulges at the "average" level of ability – the scores that most people will achieve. This is an indication, because although we *know* the average for the comparison group, we can only *assume* that this is also the average for everyone in the world who falls into the same group. Of course, statisticians come across this difficulty in

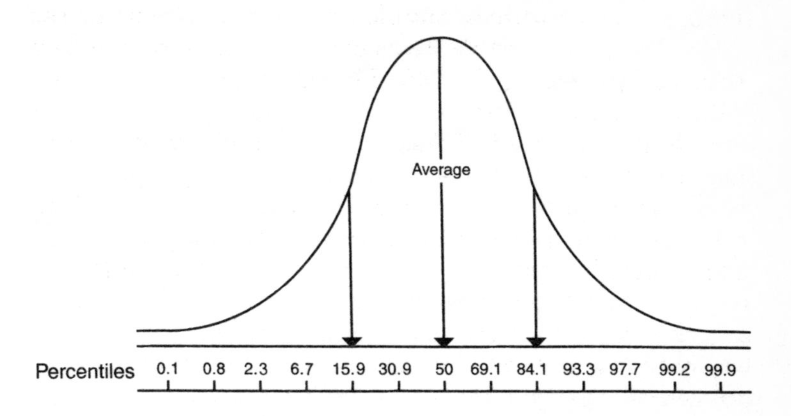

"Percentiles" show the percentage of the population tested who would obtain a particular score or lower. The "average" range extends from (roughly) the 16th to the 84th percentiles – in other words about two-thirds of the population would have scores in this range.

Fig. 12. The "Normal Distribution" – Bell-shaped curve.

many different environments, and have ways of using the data from relatively small samples to predict the picture we would get if we were to have the opportunity of testing everyone! However, it is worth remembering that the fact that ability tests are based on this statistical model makes them a different kind of instrument from, for example, a typing test. We might know that the typist needs to be able to type at a rate of a certain number of words per minute to be able to cope with the workload. The fact that this is faster or slower than the average may not be of interest.

Most ability tests cover just one kind of problem. Even where there are different kinds of question, they will be related in some way – for instance, they all require you to use logic to come up with an answer. People who are very good at that kind of problem will usually be more accurate and also faster – so they will have time to try more questions – than those who are not so good. This may seem obvious – like saying that people who are taller can reach further. But remember we are talking about mental abilities that cannot be seen except by the results when they are applied.

Many jobs have complicated demands that are not as easily measured directly as typing ability. The mental abilities that are of interest to an employer might represent a combination of skills – such as numerical problem solving plus exercising judgment where there are many different variables to be taken into account. The ability test you might be asked to complete by this employer might therefore appear not to be related to the kind of work you would be doing if appointed, but there should nevertheless be a rationale for using it.

Why Use Ability Tests?

Employers are trying to predict how well you would perform. They therefore look for a kind of measure that is likely to assist in making that prediction. In choosing a test, they might have gone through one of the following processes:

- Current employees doing similar work may have been tested using the instrument you are being asked to complete. It has been shown that the good performers in the job also tend to do better on the test. The test is therefore considered to be a useful predictor of performance. An example is a test of numerical problem solving used by a finance department to recruit accountancy trainees.
- An analysis may have been made of the skills needed to do the job, and an estimate made of the level of performance required for success. This measure is then translated into a test result, so that candidates would need to achieve at least that to be successful. For example, for an editorial job that requires a high degree of accuracy in the use and understanding of language, you might be asked to undertake a test of verbal ability.

Many jobs have complicated demands that are not easily measured directly.

- A test may have been adopted because the items in it – that is, the questions it poses – seem to relate closely to the types of decisions the job-holder would need to make. An example here is of a law firm selecting trainee solicitors and using a test of critical reasoning to see if you can make decisions objectively based on data. Another would be the aptitude tests used to recruit programmers, where the tests tap into a particular kind of logical reasoning using symbols.

- A judgment might have been made that you need to be very intelligent to be successful at the job, and a test of problem solving ability is used to see how intelligent you are. For instance, if you would be expected to undertake complex training or obtain a higher qualification, an employer might want to know that you would not find the intellectual demands too great. There is a fairly high correlation between performance on tests of problem solving and tests of general intelligence - but the latter are seldom used in employment situations because they lack what is known as "face validity". In other words, it would be hard to make a connection between the test and the job.

Employers must have a reason for including ability tests in their selection procedures, and the test must therefore have a connection to the job - even if that connection is not immediately obvious to you when you do it. There should also be a rationale for setting a "pass mark" if there is one. Otherwise they would leave themselves open to being charged with unfair discrimination, and indeed there have been cases where employers have been taken to task for using tests that did not relate to the job, or where they were setting a pass mark that could not be justified.

Are Tests Fair?

If the test truly relates to the job, it should be a very fair way of assessing candidates. No-one would say that a typing test was unfair to women, or unfair to people from different ethnic backgrounds. We would even acknowledge that it was fair to ask people with physical disabilities to take a typing test, and to use the result as a way of assessing their suitability for a typing job. It is harder to make a judgment as to whether an ability test is fairly used. If we could be confident that an ability test was as good a predictor of performance as a more direct job measure, there would be no difficulty. However, any test that is not a direct method - like an ability test - is not sufficient to be used by itself to make a prediction, and therefore to make a decision. That is why you are likely to find that the test is one of a number of different exercises you are asked to take part in.

Equally, with the exception of the more direct and specific tests, there should be the possibility of taking account of other factors when interpreting the result. You might just fail to meet the desired standard on the test, but you could have complementary strengths that compensate. People who are expected to manage a team might get by without being the best problem solvers if they are willing to involve other people and use their abilities.

It is not intended to give you an in-depth understanding of how tests are constructed and interpreted. However, you may find it reassuring to know that most tests are strictly controlled, and the ones you are likely to be faced with almost certainly will fall into this category. They can only be used by people who have been properly trained and who have enough understanding of statistics to be able to interpret the results in context. Indeed, they will have had to pass a test to qualify them to use and interpret the tests!

They will have had to pass a test to qualify them to use and interpret the tests!

What the Experience will be like

Ability tests are usually administered in a standard way. This means that the instructions are prescribed and the person who asks you to complete the test must stick to the same form of words and explanations. The reason for this is that your result will be compared to the range of results obtained by a reference group, and if you are instructed in a different way this can make that comparison spurious.

The test will almost certainly be in printed form, although some are now available to be done on a computer. You will be told where to write your answers, which may be in the form of a multiple choice response. Some tests will be computer scored, so you will be asked to make your responses in a way that the computer can read – usually by filling in circles. Manual scoring often involves placing a template over your answer sheet. In either case, it is important that your responses are in the correct place!

In tests where you are asked to put in your own answer without having a range of options from which to choose, you will be told where on the answer sheet to write your answer. In may seem very obvious that you have to make sure you put the response in the right place, but it is easy to make mistakes and put the answer to question number 15 in the space for number 16!

There is often a short practice test to get you used to the format, and the test administrator will give you the answers to those after you have had a go at them. Most ability tests are timed, and you will sometimes be told that there are more questions than most people can answer in the time. You might wonder why there should be more questions than it is possible to answer in the time allowed! Remember that the test has to be able to show a difference in performance between people who are very able and those who are not so able. For a test to be useful it has to produce a spread of results.

Test instructions have to be given in a standard way, so they are often read out. This does not mean that the people administering the test don't know what they are doing!

Actually it is more likely to mean the opposite. They are making sure that they are really being fair to you and giving you exactly the same instructions as everyone else. However, it often makes the experience seem very formal and perhaps scary – more so when you are being timed. Some people describe it as like being back at school doing exams. This is emphasised when you are not allowed to ask questions once the test has started, and you might be seated so that you cannot easily see other people's answers.

If you are someone who gets nervous during exams or under time pressure, the chances are you are going to feel the same way when you are asked to take an ability test. Most test administrators are aware that this is a stressful experience, and they will do all they can to put you at your ease – short of telling you the answers of course!

Many tests are scored by just counting correct responses, and so if you are not sure about the correct answer a guess does no harm. Some, however, have penalties for incorrect responses. The instructions may not make it clear if this is the case, so it is probably best to restrict guessing to where you are nearly certain. Where the test gives you several options, a "multiple choice" test, you can improve your chances of making a correct guess by first eliminating the ones you are sure are wrong.

Being Prepared

It is possible to improve your performance with practice, although the amount of improvement is perhaps not as great as you might think. The test is measuring a mental ability and you will get to a stage where you cannot do any better no matter how hard you try. One estimate puts the improvement it is possible to achieve with practice at around 10%. Some of this will be because you are more familiar with the type of test and therefore you use your time more efficiently, and only a part of it will be due to improved accuracy. You are unlikely to have access to the tests that will be used – they are controlled carefully and not available for general purchase. Even if you have seen the test before, perhaps at a previous selection event, you won't know which questions you got right, so in reality the practice effect is limited. However, you may be more confident about being able to do your best on the day if you know what you are likely to be faced with.

In some instances you may be told in advance what kind of ability test you will be asked to complete. You might even be sent some sample questions so that you know what to expect. If you are not told what type of test, and you have not done ability tests before, it is a good idea to try a few at home. Try tests of different types – those that require you to write in answers as well as multiple choice which require you to select from a set of possible responses. The selection process might involve a test of verbal, numerical or more abstract problem solving, and it is possible that questions of all three types might be presented together in a single test.

Your preparation is to help you do as well as you can – as has been said before, practice will improve your performance, but not beyond what you are capable of doing. As most tests are done with a strict time limit, it is worth getting used to pacing yourself so that you do not spend too much time on one question and thereby leave less time to answer questions you could have answered correctly.

At the end of this chapter are some questions that you can use for practice. If you want to do more practice, there are many books of tests available in bookshops. However, remember that the tests you are likely to meet at a selection event will never be made freely available to the public. They are restricted to those who have been trained and are registered with the publishers.

Getting Feedback

Whether successful or not in your application, if you have taken a psychometric test you will probably be interested to know how you did. Many companies are sympathetic to this and will give you some information if you ask. If they are prepared to give you some information, you will need to know not just how well you did, but also the group you are being compared against – this is known as the "norm group". For instance, you might be told that your score was average, but unless you know the reference group, that information is incomplete. You will want to know if you are being compared with the population at large, or just graduates, or managers, or current good performers.

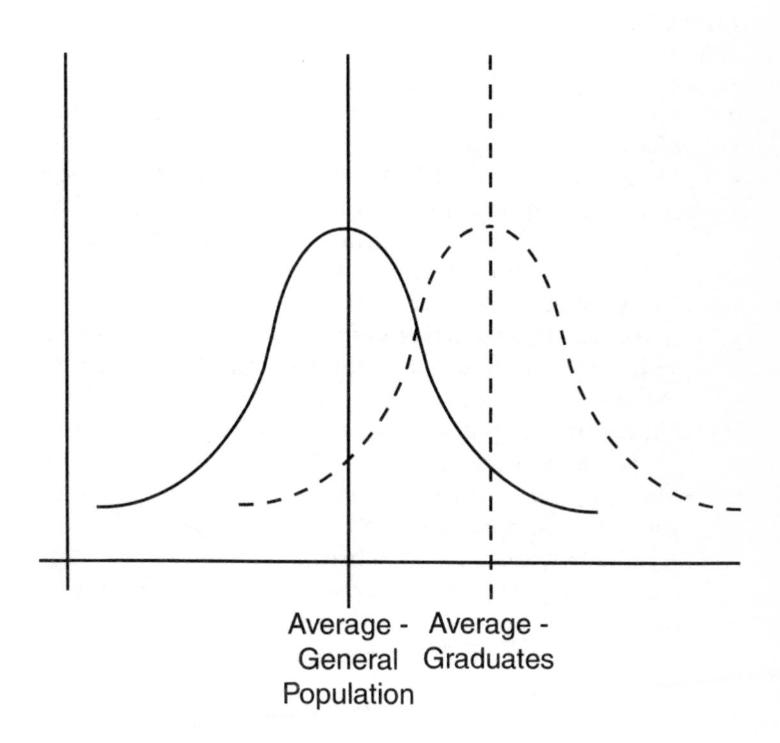

A test score is related to the "average" for a specific reference group. The same score can be "above average" for the General Population and "average" for Graduates.

Fig. 13. Graph showing difference between "average" for different groups.

Having this information can be helpful if you have to take a psychometric test in the future. Let's say that you are disappointed with your performance - maybe it is less than you would have expected given other data you have about your abilities. This may tell you that your test-taking technique is at fault, or that you were so nervous that it affected your performance. Here are some tips on taking ability tests and avoiding some common pitfalls.

Tips for Doing Ability Tests

- Try to get some practice before you attend a selection event - do different kinds of tests and rehearse completing them under time pressure.
- Make sure you understand the instructions before you start - ask questions to get clarification at the time you are given the instructions or after you have done the example questions. You won't be able to ask once you have started the real test.
- If you get the examples wrong, concentrate on seeing what you did that was wrong rather than trying to prove that you were right - you weren't!
- Skim through the test and do questions that are easy for you straightaway.
- Manage your time actively - decide how long you can afford to spend on each question and make a judgment early about whether to leave it or struggle on. Spending a few extra seconds and getting it right is fine. Spending all your time allowance, before you decide you're never going to get there, is a bad idea.
- Don't be discouraged if there are a few questions you can't do. Just move on to one that you can.
- If you find yourself getting nervous or panic stricken, pause and concentrate on your breathing for a few seconds - it will use up some of your time, but will help you calm down and do a better job with the time you have left.

- Be careful about where you write your responses – make sure you keep track of the question number and write your answer in the correct place. It is easy to get out of step if you've missed a question.
- Be especially careful if you have time to check your responses. Many mistakes are made when people change right answers to wrong ones at this stage! You might be better spending time on questions you haven't been able to do than returning to ones you were happy with first time round.

Summary

This chapter took you through what ability tests are and why they are used. It also offered some guidance as to how you can approach them so that you can do as well as you can. Some examples of the kinds of questions that you might meet in ability tests are included on the next few pages to give you some practice, but if you are not familiar with tests you are encouraged to get some more practice with timed tests.

Sample Ability Test

"Reasoning" means working something out by thinking about it. A "verbal" reasoning test looks at how you work things out when the information you are given is in the form of words – rather than numbers or abstract symbols. This is not the same as a test of verbal ability – such as how wide your vocabulary is or how well you understand words – but there is a relationship. If you find the language of the test difficult, you are less likely to be able to work out the problem and respond quickly.

A common way of testing verbal reasoning is to give you some information and then ask questions that require you to use your judgment based on that information. The questions might be in the form of a statement, and you have to decide whether the statement is true and follows logically from the information given.

Here is an example:

Read the following paragraph, then decide whether the statements below are likely to be:

(a) True.
(b) Untrue.
(c) Cannot decide.

Mrs Lewis is a respected teacher of English, whose students usually get good grades in their "A" level examinations. She is strongly of the opinion that students should be exposed to as many forms of the material as possible, and she frequently uses films and stage performances as teaching tools.

1. Mrs Lewis is an excellent teacher – that's why her students get good grades.
2. Students in Mrs Lewis' class are likely to see performances of the plays they are studying.
3. Other teachers have been critical of Mrs Lewis' teaching methods.

In the example given, the correct responses would be 1 (c), 2(a), 3(b). Although Mrs Lewis may be an excellent teacher, there could be other reasons for her students getting good grades – they may be very bright or have additional tuition outside school. So the first statement may be either true or untrue – you cannot decide for sure on the basis of the information given. However, statement 2 is likely to be true – you are told that she not only believes in this method but also frequently uses it. Statement 3 is likely to be untrue. You have no evidence in the paragraph that it is true, and the fact that she is "respected" suggests that it is probably untrue.

You need to make sure you understand the instructions for the particular test – some allow you to use common knowledge when responding, but you could be asked to use only the information given.

In the following sample ability test you will find four others like the one shown above. The rest of the test covers different kinds of items, and you will need to read the description and instructions for each.

As a practice, you might want to work through all 12 examples as if you were under time pressure. If you want to do this, allow yourself 40 minutes. You will need pencils or a pen, paper for rough working and a separate sheet to record your answers. For some of the items you will need a calculator. Have all this ready, together with a stop-watch or kitchen timer so that you can see how far you get in 40 minutes.

The answers are all on pages 110-111. Try not to look at them before you have finished the test.

Don't be discouraged if you make some mistakes. It is very rare for anyone to complete an ability test and get everything right! In fact, many tests are constructed so that only a few people can finish them in the time allowed. Remember that all the other candidates are in the same position, and if you find some items hard then the chances are that many other people will also have difficulty.

For each of the first four examples, read the paragraph, then decide whether the statements below it are likely to be:

(a) True.
(b) Untrue.
(c) Cannot decide.

Example 1

June and Peter are getting married in the summer. June wants a quiet wedding with as little fuss as possible, but her parents will be disappointed if their only daughter gets married without a big party. They also feel that if they are paying for it they should have some say in what happens. Peter has said that he does not care, but has given way over other things and this time he does not want to be held to ransom by June's parents. He has suggested that they pay for their own wedding and if June's parents want to make a party that is up to them. So far this seems like an acceptable solution.

1. June and Peter's wedding is likely to be postponed.
2. June is an only child.
3. Peter is used to getting his own way.

Example 2

Lakeland Properties is a company specialising in holiday lets in Europe. It owns and manages many delightful and remote lakeside houses located where there is dramatic scenery. Luxury and space are key features of the properties, which range from two-bedroomed cottages to 20-roomed mansions. Catering for the upper end of the market, transport is provided door to door and guests complete a questionnaire in advance to select the kinds of food and drink they would like to have ready for them so that they have supplies for their first day when they arrive. Most guests are so pleased with their holiday that they recommend Lakeland Properties to their friends and repeat bookings are very common.

1. The largest property on Lakeland's books has 20 bedrooms.
2. Guests have no need to shop for food during their holiday.
3. Lakeland is able to rely on "word of mouth" for much of its marketing.

Example 3

An insurance company published information about the drivers of vehicles involved in accidents based on claims made by their customers. Approximately two-thirds of the accidents involved male drivers. The drivers most likely to be the cause of accidents were between 17 and 21 years old, and in this age-group there are many more male than female drivers. A company representative stated "We have adjusted our premiums so that from now on those with the most chance of being involved in an accident pay more. We believe this is fair to everyone."

1. Most accidents are caused by male drivers.
2. Female drivers are likely to pay less with this company than with other companies.
3. In the past, premiums did not reflect the probability of being involved in an accident.

Example 4

If you were to ask most people what they do in their leisure time, the response might be sport, going to pubs and restaurants, visiting friends or watching television. Few would cite shopping as a leisure pursuit, but when you look how people actually spend their time off, a large part of it is in shops. Even when you remove the time they shop for food, shopping seems to be a large part of many people's lives.

1. Pubs and restaurants have become less popular as a way of spending leisure time.
2. Most people don't think of shopping as a leisure activity.
3. Many people lie when asked about how they spend their time.

The next two problems are examples of numerical reasoning items. Here the problem requires you to undertake some numerical analysis to come up with answers to the questions. In these examples you are given tables of figures, but you could also be asked to use information presented as graphs or charts. **You can use a calculator** for these examples.

Example 5

The following table shows sales for the first quarter of a company's financial year by each of the four sales teams – the team leader's name is given in the table. The figures represent units sold.

MONTH	**April**	**May**	**June**
SALES REP			
Jones	404	578	609
Davidson	471	599	602
McDowell	418	497	540
Singh	460	584	598

Additional information:

- Team bonuses are paid when targets are exceeded in each quarter.
- Each unit represents £30 profit, and the team bonus is 25% of the profit for each unit above target.

1. Which sales team had the highest performance during the period shown?
2. Sales for this group were up 20% on last year's figures. What was the total for last year?
3. McDowell's team had a target of 400 in April, 520 in May and 550 in June. How many more units would they have needed to sell to achieve a bonus in this quarter?
4. Jones' team had the same targets as McDowell's. What team bonus did they achieve?
5. Sales for the 2nd quarter usually show a monthly figure around the same level as June. However, a marketing initiative is hoped to bring in 10% more sales for August. What figure should we expect for the total sales in the 2nd quarter?

Example 6

A company analysed its expenditure on various items as a first step to introducing some cost-cutting measures. Costs relate to the previous calendar year. It is now March.

Item	Expenditure in $
Phone charges	4,386
Post and carriage	2,784
Stationery	1,300
Travel expenses	18,750
Entertaining	8,640

Additional information:

- Last year's rental on the phone was $350 and this year will be the same. Call charges have been reduced by 5%.
- The cost of postage last year was $1,104. "Carriage" costs refer to items sent by courier at a per item cost of $7. The courier has increased charges for the current year by $1 per item, whilst post costs remain the same.
- Travel expenses will rise by 5% this year if the same amount of travel is undertaken.

Give all answers to the nearest $.

1. The company expects phone usage to reduce by 15% because of the increased use of e-mail. What figure should they budget for in the current year?
2. The same number of items has to be sent each month, either by post or courier. However, from 1st April, 25% of items previously sent by courier will be posted instead, at a cost of $1 per item. How much less will be spent on "Post and Carriage" this year?
3. All employees have been asked to restrict travel and to use economy fares wherever feasible. This should cut $4,980 from the total cost over the current year at last year's prices. What will the new budget figure be for this year?
4. Stationery prices have increased by 5%, but there is some stock so that less will be purchased this year than last year. It is estimated that the stock represents 2 months' usage. What will the company spend on stationery this year?
5. Entertaining includes an annual party. This year the cost is likely to be $1,360. Other entertaining expenses are under the control of 20 employees. What maximum allowance can each person be given to reduce the year's cost by $1,000?

Tests of verbal ability require you to use your knowledge of words and your understanding of their meaning to answer the questions. They can take many different forms. The following three examples test your verbal ability.

Example 7

Sample:
rising (star) performer

For each of the following, insert the word that relates to each of the other two in the same way as the sample item. (Clue: The number of dots tells you how many letters make up the word.)

(a) first (. . . . . .) ceremony
(b) tea (. . .) plant
(c) silver (. . . . .) glass
(d) swimming (. . . .) table

Example 8

Sample:

Egg is to Chicken as Tadpole is to:
Animal Pond Kitten Frog Fish

Select the correct word from the selection given:

(a) Blue is to Colour as Dog is to:
Cat Animal Kennel Horse Fog

(b) Gain is to Loss as Forward is to:
Car Point South Reverse Down

(c) Travel is to Plane as Decorate is to:
Leisure Paint Sport Home Spend

(d) When is to Today as Where is to:
Why Now Here Tomorrow Place

Example 9

Which word in the group on the right means the same as each of the following?

(a)	*Generous*	Stingy	Magnificent	Munificent	Ample
(b)	*Felon*	Animal	Criminal	Cannibal	Picture
(c)	*Censure*	Edit	Suppress	Reprimand	Heat
(d)	*Order*	Find	Attend	Object	Rank

The next three examples are based on logic.

Example 10

In each row you are given a series of numbers or letters, and you have to decide what comes next in the series.

(a)	.4	1.2	3.6	10.8	?
(b)	12	15	18	21	?
(c)	4	8	16	32	?
(d)	C	E	H	L	?
(e)	14620	41620	46120	46210	?
(f)	10	11	100	101	?

Example 11

The upper two items have a feature in common. Which **one** item in the group below has the same feature?

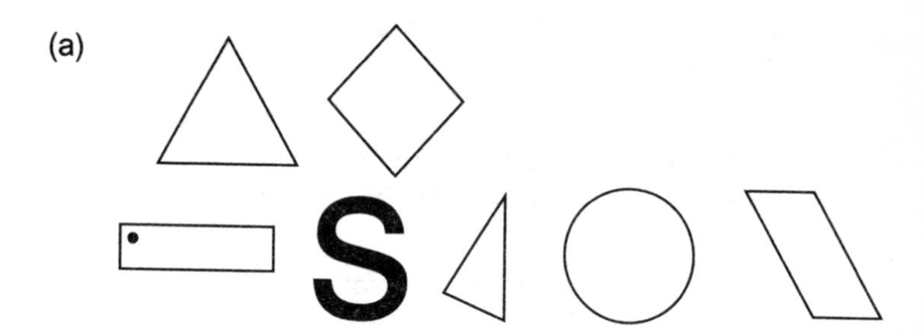

(b) e Z

X C U A $

(c)

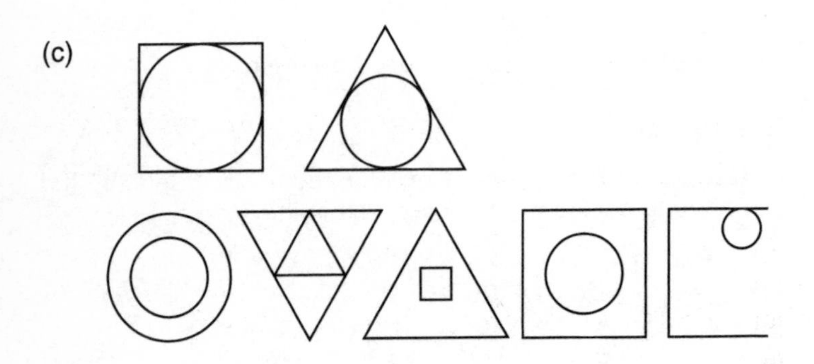

(d)

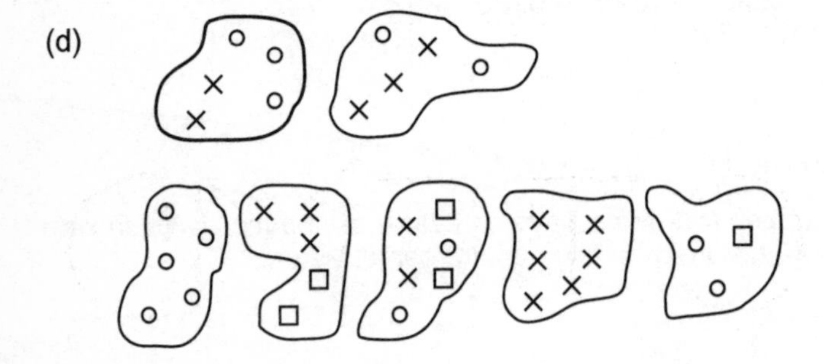

(e)

Example 12

In each of the rows below there is one which does not fit with the rest. ***Pick the odd one out.***

(a)

(b)

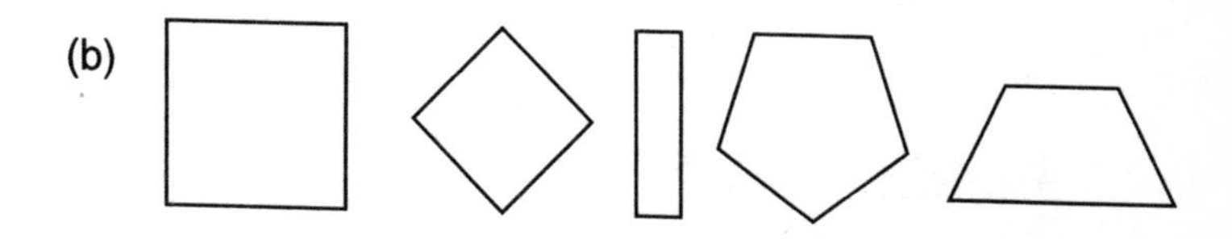

(c)

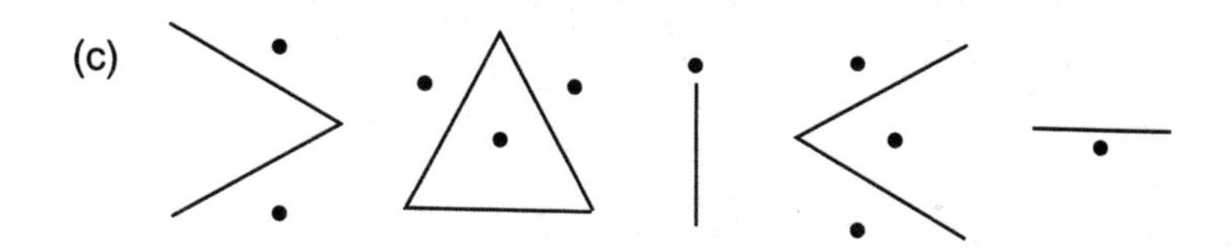

(d)

(e)

Answers

1.	1(b)	2(c)	3(c)
2.	1(b)	2(b)	3(a)
3.	1(a)	2(c)	3(a)
4.	1(c)	2(a)	3(c)
5.	1. Davidson	2. £5,300	3. 16
	4. £907.50	5. £7,282	
6.	1. $3,609	2. $75	3. $14,459
	4. $1,138	5. $314	
7.	(a) degree	(b) pot	(c) plate
	(d) pool		
8.	(a) Animal	(b) Reverse	(c) Paint
	(d) Here		
9.	(a) Munificent	(b) Criminal	(c) Reprimand
	(d) Rank		
10.	(a) 32.4	(b) 24	(c) 64
	(d) Q	(e) 46201	(f) 110

11. (a) 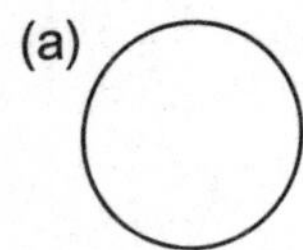
(b) 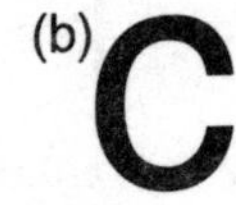
(c) 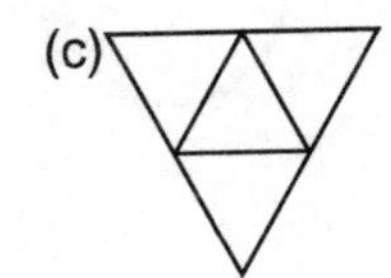
(d) 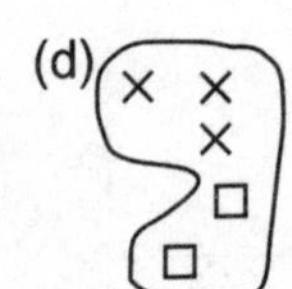
(e) 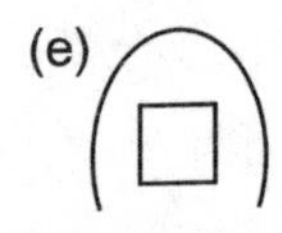

12. (a)  (b) 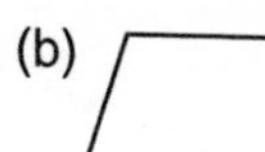 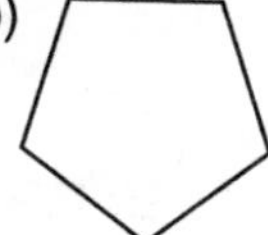 (c) 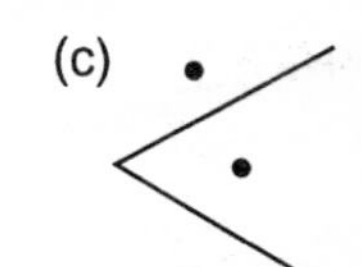

(d) 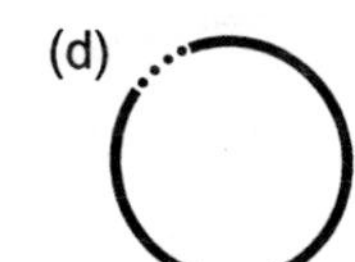 (e) 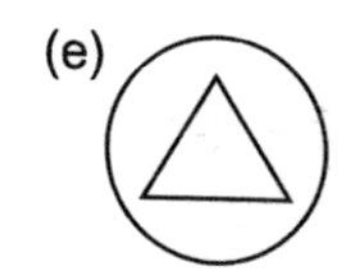

Chapter 7:

Assessment Centres

What is an Assessment Centre?

If you are asked to attend an "Assessment Centre", you are likely to have a range of different activities throughout the day, possibly including the types of tests described in the previous chapters. "Assessment Centre" is a piece of jargon referring to any assessment event that has the following characteristics:

- Assessment is by more than one method.
- Assessment is made by more than one person.
- Usually, assessment will be against a set of criteria.

This means that an interview alone would not constitute an Assessment Centre. However, an interview can form part of one when put together with some other exercises, such as psychometric tests and a group discussion. Similarly, you will know that there is going to be more than one person assessing your qualities and characteristics, so you are not just trying to impress one person. These different observations will be brought together in order to reach a decision.

Assessment Centres are regarded as "best practice" because they help to make decisions fair and objective. Typically the observers will have been trained to look for specific behaviours, characteristics, competences or experiences that help them to assess your ability to do the job.

This chapter takes you through some commonly used types of exercises.

The ones covered here are:

- Group exercises – various different types.
- In-tray (sometimes called "in-basket").
- Simulations.
- Presentations – either prepared in advance or on the day.
- Graphology.
- The guided tour.

Assessment Centres help make decisions fair and objective.

As with the tests, which may form part of an Assessment Centre, each exercise will have a reason for being included. The assessment will be made either by observation and judgment, or by reference to a "model answer", or some combination of the two. The next chapter looks more specifically at the interview, which might be an element of an Assessment Centre, or, of course, could stand alone.

Group Exercises

Many jobs require us to work with other people, and Assessment Centres therefore often include an exercise that requires interaction with other candidates. Sometimes this will relate quite closely to the type of work you would be required to do, but not always. If the exercise does relate to the work, it may be that your expertise is being assessed as well as your ability to work well with other people. Some jobs attract candidates from a wide range of backgrounds, and someone who was already familiar with the kind of work might be expected to do well at such an exercise, whereas someone without that experience might find that they are learning as they go along.

One way of avoiding the difference that exists just because of experience is to use an exercise that does not relate to the job at all, but has some features that are important for good performance. These exercises might be creative or require problem solving with limited resources.

The exercise will have been designed to elicit the characteristics that the company thinks are important for success in the job, and it will be those characteristics that the observers will be particularly interested in when they are watching you and taking notes. This is the case whether or not the exercise has similarities with the job itself.

The types of qualities and characteristics commonly being observed during group exercises include the following:

- **Influencing** – How far are you able to get other people to see things your way and agree with you? How do you persuade them? Do other members of the group tend to listen to you?
- **Impact** – Do you earn respect from other group members? Can you ensure that you are heard even when others are keen to have their say? Do you appear confident?
- **Communication skills** – Are you sufficiently articulate? Can you express your ideas in a way that makes them accessible to other people? Do you keep to the point?
- **Quality of ideas** – Do you add intellectually to the discussion? Do you pitch your views at the right level –

not too obvious and not too way out? Are you clearly on top of the topic?

- **Handling disagreement** - Do you avoid destructive conflict? Can you raise disagreements without upsetting or demotivating others in the group? Do you refrain from backing down just to get consensus - without getting in the way of reaching an agreement? Can you help resolve differences of view?
- **Judgment** - Do you appear to know when to speak and when to listen? Do you pick up good ideas and avoid poorer ones? Can you draw attention to the key issues and not be sidetracked by "red herrings"?
- **Leadership** - Do you take charge and control the process of the discussion or task? Do you act as the "chair"? Can you help others to make a contribution? Do you summarise the current position and identify next steps?
- **Teamwork** - Do you acknowledge others' different strengths and abilities? Do you help the others in the group to clarify their thoughts or ideas? Can you keep everyone involved? Do you offer support?
- **Appropriate social behaviour** - Do you apologise for interrupting? Is your language appropriate to the situation? Does your body language suggest that you are interested and paying attention? Can you make a distinction between times when it is appropriate to be lighthearted and when you need to be more serious?
- **Results focus** - Do you make sure there are clear objectives? Are you eager to get to the required outcome? Do you manage time well so that the task is finished? Do you avoid getting distracted by peripheral issues? Can you determine which items need more discussion and which can be cut short?

This is a long list, and no exercise will cover even half the items on it. However, most will cover two or three as targeted characteristics so that observers will be looking specifically for evidence that shows you either have or have not enough to make you acceptable. Some characteristics, even if not targeted, can be negatively assessed if you behave in a way that causes the observers some concern. For instance, *being polite* might not be on the observers' list of things to watch for, but they will certainly notice if you are rude to other participants. They might not have been asked to assess your *level of concentration*, but if you appear to be more interested in writing your shopping list than participating in the exercise this will not go down well!

You can be negatively assessed if you behave in a way that causes observers some concern.

What will the Experience be like?

You will probably be in a group of between three and eight people. The others in the group will be candidates, just as you are, and this may arouse your competitive instincts. For discussion exercises you are likely to be seated round a table, perhaps with notepads in front of you, and there may be a flipchart for the group to use. Or you could be seated in a circle without tables, or asked to work in a room with some materials and no chairs or tables.

Someone will explain what you are required to do, and how long you have for the exercise. You might have a written brief to look at. Bear in mind that in some exercises your brief might be different from everyone else's, for instance if you are asked to take a particular role, or if the exercise demands that different people have access to different information.

You might feel strange at first because you are being watched and it is often the case that there will be more than one observer. Each observer will be concentrating mainly on one or two people, but will obviously pick up information about the group as a whole. Don't feel that you have to include the observers in anything you do, unless you are specifically asked to do so. It is not a good idea to address comments to observers - they want you to treat them as if they were part of the wallpaper. Most people find that after a short time they are able to forget about the observers and concentrate on the exercise.

Group Discussions

Many group exercises take the form of a discussion. These group discussion exercises can be open-ended - where you are given a topic to talk about as a group. Alternatively, they might have a specified end point - a solution to be offered to a problem or an agreed next step to a scenario. You might be asked to read something first and spend some time thinking about the topic in preparation for the discussion. Even if the topic does not appear to be directly related to the job you are being assessed for, it is likely that it has been chosen to give an opportunity to show characteristics that are relevant to the job.

In choosing the topic, the assessors will have decided whether they are looking at your work-related experience, or whether they want to avoid looking at this. They might want to avoid it if they are prepared to provide training, and therefore don't want to disadvantage someone with less experience, but more potential. However, if it is very important that the person they appoint has, say, a good knowledge of competitors, the exercise might provide the opportunity to demonstrate that.

An Open-ended Discussion

In an open-ended discussion, there is no specified goal for the group. You will be given some information - which might be only a headline, or as much as several pages - to read before the group starts to talk. The topic might be taken from a current news item, a competitor's advertisement, or a theme of relevance to the industry or the community. If the topic is close to the job, the content might be assessed as well as the process. For instance, this might be a way of assessing your level of knowledge, interest and motivation. Sometimes it might be chosen to engender debate around a controversial issue - to see how you handle disagreement, take a position or listen to views other than your own.

It would be difficult to avoid trying to guess what the observers are looking for. However, trying to second guess them may make you perform worse rather than better. It could make you more anxious and self-conscious, or encourage you to act a part rather than being yourself.

Obviously, it is important to give the observers some data! If you say nothing throughout, all they can do is comment on your demeanour and body language, which is unlikely to be enough to make a judgment on your interpersonal skills, your influencing or your level of drive and motivation.

Group Problem-solving Exercises

A group exercise might take the form of a problem to be solved. In this you are likely to be given information about something that has gone wrong or where action needs to be taken. Only rarely will there be a single answer to the problem, and you will certainly know if this is the case. The more likely situation is that there will be several possible solutions, all of which have their own difficulties.

The possible solutions might include some that should be avoided, or only adopted with some acknowledgement of the risks involved. Your ability to decide on a course of action, taking into account the implications that result from your chosen action, will be of interest to the observers.

Again, the problem to be solved may not appear to be related directly to the job. You may feel that you are being asked to work on something that you have little or no experience of. Don't be put off by this. If you feel like that, the chances are that the other candidates are in a similar position. It will be recognised that people come from different backgrounds and have different experiences to draw on. Remember that group exercises are almost always included to give an indication of how you interact with others, such as how much you listen and contribute, how you are able to influence or how you support and collaborate.

Goal or Outcome Focused Exercises

In some instances the group exercise may be more creative or constructional, in which case the process of achieving the end point will be assessed more than the end point itself. For example, if you are asked as a group to construct a paper tower, the quality of the tower is less likely to be of interest than the process you, as a group participant, went through in deciding what it would look like, how to build it and who would do what.

There are many different versions of group exercises where the group has to achieve a specific goal or outcome including:

- Constructing something - such as a tower made of a restricted assortment of materials.
- Designing an advertisement for a product or recruitment campaign.
- A physical activity to get the group to a different place following a set of rules or using specific equipment.

- Creating a new product or service.

These exercises can be a lot of fun, but they can also be quite stressful if you don't regard yourself as especially creative or lateral in your thinking. You might feel a bit awkward being asked to use materials that seem more appropriate to nursery school, or self-conscious if you feel that your lack of talent is being exposed. The thing to remember is that these exercises are usually designed to level the playing field. They specifically don't rely on what you are most practised at, and even if you are very good at cutting out shapes or making towers out of paper, it is unlikely to be that ability that will get you the job!

Let's take the issue of creativity as an example of how you might be assessed. Being naturally creative might be seen as an advantage, but if you are unable to prioritise your ideas, or fail to let go of ones that would take too long to implement, you could be seen as more of a liability than as an asset to the group. If your style is more concrete and analytical, and you seldom indulge in creative pursuits, this need not be a handicap unless you also demotivate the others in the group by being disparaging about their ideas or if you hold them back by refusing to take a risk. Creativity *per se* is therefore not the issue. It is the ability to generate or nurture creative solutions that are also practical ones. Participants who are supportive and show appreciation of others' ideas, and perhaps also help to shape the less practical ones to make them usable, will be viewed positively.

Competitive Exercises

Occasionally you might be asked to take part in an exercise as part of a team competing against another team. Of course, the teams will be made up of other candidates for the job. The task might be to accomplish something in less time than the other team, or to produce a better result. Any of the above goal/outcome focused exercises could be run in this way, for instance your cardboard

"Yes, but it will never fly."

Don't demotivate the others in the group by disparaging their ideas.

tower might be judged in terms of height or stability, and your task would be to make it higher and more stable than that of the other team. Don't be distracted by this! The judgment of the tower is not the same as the judgment of you. A competitive element is introduced for a variety of reasons, which may include:

- Determining how important quality is to you - some people get so involved in reaching an end result that they compromise too much on quality.
- Assessing your ability to make objective judgments, even when they are self-critical - whether you are able to acknowledge that someone else's idea is better than yours.
- Evaluating your ability to inspire and motivate others to achieve a better result - if you can help the team to get a result that is beyond your personal capability.

- Looking at how you learn from competitors – how you draw on what different people are doing when looking for new ways of achieving the best result.

The main thing to remember is that winning in this instance is unlikely to be what gets you the job, but wanting to win and showing that you know why you won, or how you could have done better, might be very important.

Approaching Group Exercises

Group exercises pose a particular difficulty because you are working with people who are also trying to get the job you want. Of course, there may be more than one position, but even so it is difficult to avoid thinking that the other people in the group are opponents rather than members of your team. If you do something to help them, are you also reducing your own chances of getting the job? If you appear to support them, does that suggest that you didn't have better or different ideas of your own? If, on the other hand, you fail to support them, will this be seen as "sour grapes" rather than your genuine belief that there's a better way of doing something?

Your approach to a group exercise will certainly be observed. The exercise has been included because the way you interact is seen as important by those making the selection decision.

Because every group is different, there is no blueprint for success. How then do you ensure that you do your best in a group discussion? There are some common sense things to bear in mind, such as basic courtesy, being polite and showing consideration for the others in the group. However some things might be more specific to you, and here you will benefit by being aware of how other people typically see you.

One way is to think about how you usually behave in groups, and the impact of your behaviour. Maybe you have had feedback in the past about how you work with groups that helps you see what is effective and what could be improved. If you take such feedback seriously, it will apply to other situations and not just when you are at an Assessment Centre, but it is helpful to remind yourself about what is likely to emerge under stress. If you are unsure about this, talk to friends and family who know you well and can be trusted to be honest with you. What are your faults when you are discussing or working in a group? Do you tend to interrupt, ignore some people, use "bad" language or come across as too critical? And what about the things you do that are helpful and effective? Do you ask questions, draw attention to others' good ideas or explain complex things simply?

You might want to construct a list of reminders - but here is one to help you get started:

- Speak clearly - don't mumble.
- Look at everyone in the group but especially the person who's speaking.
- Try to be polite - if you have to interrupt do it tactfully.
- Show support more than disagreement - if you have to disagree try to take the other person's feelings into account.
- Show appreciation and listening by referring to what others have said.
- Be a participant, not an observer - your assessors need data to make their decision.
- Have a conversation, don't make a speech.
- Make eye contact with more than one person when talking.
- If there's a clear end-point, keep on the task (the problem to be solved, the objective to be achieved) - but not to the point of failing to explore options.
- Be open to others - listen without being judgmental.
- Create space for your contribution (I'd like to add a point; I have a question; Can I put a different view?; Could we return to X's point?).
- Don't "play to the gallery" - observers will not be impressed if you attend to them rather than to the other participants.

Everyone has their own strengths and weaknesses in groups. The more you know about yours, the better you can deploy your strengths appropriately and mitigate your weaknesses - and this refers to all occasions where you might be involved with groups, not just when being assessed. Be prepared to critique your performance - sometimes you will be asked about the group exercise in a later interview. You will impress more by an honest appraisal, especially if you also show willingness to adapt.

Other Assessment Activities and Exercises

Apart from group exercises, you might be asked to undertake any of the following activities, all of which are used in assessing candidates. Given that most Assessment Centres take place on one day, and that there will generally be an interview taking up part of the time, the number of different exercises is necessarily limited. This section is to give you some examples of what you might face. I have included graphology more for information rather than to give guidance - it is a technique seldom used in the UK, USA or Australia, but favoured in some European countries. I have also included the "guided tour" which on the face of it is not an assessment activity, so that you can ensure you make good use of this opportunity.

In-tray

In-tray exercises, sometimes called "in-basket", are constructed taking real or likely issues that you might have to face if appointed. The idea is that you are given a typical in-tray with the notes, correspondence and information a real job-holder would have. The assignment associated with this in-tray is to make decisions about the course of action you would take in each case. You might be given a diary page and asked to use this to schedule the different tasks you have decided you should do.

There are two clear parts to such an exercise:

- To decide how you will deal with each of the issues.
- To prioritise them both in relation to each other and to the other items you may already have in your diary.

Just as in real life, you should bear in mind that you can cancel as well as make appointments during this exercise. For instance, you may decide that the meeting you have in your diary with a sales representative can be postponed or delegated if there is something more pressing that you should deal with.

A helpful way of thinking about each item is to consider both how much time you should be spending on it (a measure of its importance) and how soon you need to deal with it (a measure of its urgency). A crisis might be something which is both important and urgent – you need to put time aside for it, and you need to do it now! However, most things we deal with are not crises, and we have to make judgments about what we will do first and how much time we are prepared to devote to a particular issue. Sometimes we choose to do relatively trivial things quickly because we can get them out of the way, and it would take longer to brief someone else to do it.

The information you have will, of course, not be complete. In an exercise like this you cannot expect to have all the information that a real job-holder would have access to. You may therefore need to make some assumptions, for instance that there is a secretary who can assist in re-scheduling meetings, or that you can e-mail messages to your team. However, avoid making up unlikely solutions – solving a delivery problem using the company jet might not go down well!

Your in-tray might contain a mixture of "people" and "task" issues. People issues might be:

- A member of your team has complained that he is being harassed.
- Someone is on extended sick leave.

- An appointment has been requested to discuss career development.
- You have to tell an employee that she was unsuccessful in getting promotion.
- A colleague is disappointed with the performance of one of your team.

Task issues might cover:

- Equipment failure.
- A deadline which you cannot meet.
- Project review.
- Meetings with customers or suppliers.
- Faulty product.

You will have a set time to complete the exercise, and you need to ensure that you manage your time efficiently. Don't assume you have to deal personally with every item - be prepared to delegate. For instance, if there are more pressing matters, you could choose to allow the project manager to conduct the review without you, and arrange to brief you later. Where you do have to be personally involved, for instance in talking to a team member who feels he is being harassed, make sure you are realistic about how much time this will take. Exercising judgment will be called for. If you are unable to see an unhappy team member immediately, you should think about what will be an adequate "holding response".

When doing an exercise like this, think not just of the immediate task, but also of the longer term implications. For instance, you might decide that you have to halt delivery of a faulty product in the short term, but then you might want to initiate some investigation to find out why the fault occurred in this consignment and put in place measures to prevent it from happening in the future.

Your responses will probably be matched against a set of "right answers" - perhaps the exercise has been tested out using existing people in the organisation and a view taken as to the best solutions. It is less likely that the "right answers" will be the only ones judged to be suitable. You might find that you are asked questions about this exercise afterwards or in your interview. It is therefore important that you have a rationale for the decisions you have taken. You should be prepared to explain why you have made the choices you have, but also to accept that there could be a better solution than the one you have come up with. Beware of being overly wedded to your solution, which can make you seem rigid and unwilling to learn. However, also beware of being too easily swayed if your chosen solution is challenged as you could give the impression of lacking confidence in your own judgment. If this makes it seem as though you can't win, remember to be genuine. If you really believe your solution is better, and can argue your case rationally and politely, this is fine. Alternatively, if you are convinced that another solution is better, it is honest to say so.

Guidelines for In-tray Exercises

- Start with a quick scan of the items so that you can decide how to use your time efficiently.
- Be flexible in your approach. Remember you can delegate some tasks and postpone already scheduled items if necessary.
- Be sensitive to people issues - you may have to establish a holding position if you cannot give enough time to resolving them immediately.
- Consider both short term and long term - what you have to do to resolve a current situation and any longer term issues this raises.
- Make intelligent assumptions - you are not expected to know everything about the job.
- Be prepared to justify your decisions, but beware of defending them too strongly.

Simulation/Scenario

The in-tray exercise described above is an example of a simulation - where you are asked to deal with issues that could be real ones. The in-tray gives you a work sample covering varied tasks. Sometimes you will be asked to work on a single issue or scenario. In this case it is more likely that your knowledge and skill in a particular area are being assessed. Examples might be:

- Providing a commentary on a set of accounts.
- Translating sales figures into a graphical presentation.
- Working out how to move goods to different depots to meet delivery schedules.
- Planning an office move.
- Designing research into customer satisfaction.
- Dealing with a disciplinary matter.
- Assessing a site for a new store/factory.

Exercises such as these give you an opportunity to demonstrate skills and knowledge in a very direct way. Those assessing you will be able to see the accuracy of your analysis and your ability to construct a solution in the allotted time. This kind of exercise is concerned with depth rather than breadth – you are not being asked to display a wide range of capabilities, but rather to show how deeply you understand the scenario you are faced with. Often the solution will be a combination of special knowledge and common sense. The way you present your solution should demonstrate both.

Always give some thought to the people who are assessing you. What will make your response easy for them to understand? Often the answer is to build in some structure. For instance, if you are planning an office move, you might want to list the resources you will require and show a timeplan for the different activities. When assessing a site, you might decide that a "SWOT" (strengths, weaknesses, opportunities, threats) analysis will help to show the basis of your ultimate decision.

If there is time, you can also go beyond the brief – but only if you are satisfied that you have done enough in response to the exercise. Adding further value to the exercise might be to show how a labour intensive operation can be simplified, or how some knowledge-based activities can be automated.

Guidelines for Simulations/Scenarios

- Make sure you are clear about what output is expected - don't waste your time doing things that are not required.
- Make balanced judgments - if you are required to make a recommendation, don't over-sell it, but rather show that you understand the possible downsides.
- Avoid glib or sketchy responses - give the assessors enough information to assess you.
- Structure your answer so that it is easily understood.
- If you have time, add value to the result.

Presentation

As part of the assessment procedure, you may be asked to prepare a presentation. Presentations are usually included in the procedure when the assessors are interested in the way you put forward ideas and how persuasive and convincing you are, as well as the quality of the ideas themselves. Sometimes the preparation for the presentation is made before you attend, and you will be asked to bring it with you so that you can present it to the assessors on the day. If you are asked to do this, it is obviously important that you prepare for the right medium - and you should make sure you ask the right questions before attending if you are not sure exactly how you are expected to make your presentation. There's no point in putting effort into a computer generated presentation if you are expected to work just from a flipchart! Most commonly, you will be asked to use either a flipchart or overhead projector, but this could change as computer presentations become more the norm.

On other occasions, you will be given time on the day to prepare your presentation and obviously the materials you are expected to use will be provided. Whilst this type of exercise might be seen as being more fair, as all candidates are in exactly the same position, it is probably more difficult as you have less time to think about what you want to say and how you want to say it.

Whether you are preparing your presentation in advance or on the day, you will want to make a good impression. If you are not used to making presentations, or if you know that this is not an area you excel at, it is worth having some basic principles in mind when preparing. The rest of this section is designed to help you by giving guidance about how presentations are judged and how to put your ideas across effectively.

What makes a Good Presentation?

First of all, what do we mean by a **good** presentation? We make judgments about how good something is by reference to standards or criteria. For instance, a good runner might be fast; if we add that this is a good *marathon* runner then we might also consider stamina.

We judge the performance more than the effort that goes into preparation. However, to improve performance we often concentrate on preparation. With our marathon runner we might adjust the training schedule or the amount of carbohydrate consumed to reach the objectives of going the whole distance (stamina) in a given time (speed). But the runner does not get credit for a healthy diet!

When we think of a presentation, we can improve performance by being clear about the objectives and tuning preparation to achieve those objectives.

Presentation Objectives might be:

- To communicate a set of results.
- To motivate a team.
- To sell an idea.
- To teach a new technique.
- To introduce a product or person.
- To change a perception.
- To explain strategy.

– or a combination.

For your presentation, the title you are given or the area you are asked to cover will give you an indication of what your objective should be, but don't make the mistake of assuming that covering the topic is a good objective. Instead, think about how you want the assessors to think and feel at the end of it, and make that your objective.

For the runner, the achievement of objectives is easy to measure – if you have a measured track and a stopwatch. Your presentation objectives can only be measured with reference to your audience. If you want to explain an idea and the assessors are not able to understand it clearly, you have not achieved your objective. If your presentation is to impress the assessors with some technique you have used in the past, and they are bored by the presentation, you have not achieved your objective.

Given that the subject matter is only part of what you need to pay attention to, it is sometimes helpful to think of the presentation as having three components:

- The content.
- Your way of putting it across.
- The technical aids you use.

All three come together, of course, in your presentation, but each needs thinking about separately to meet your objectives. The following are suggested questions, covering each of the three areas, to ask yourself when preparing.

Content

- Have you understood the brief – is it clear what topic you intend to cover?
- Is it interesting to your audience – how can you make sure that it will be?
- Have you made sure of your facts?
- Are you pitching the presentation at the right level – not too easy or complicated?
- Is quantity of material appropriate to the time available?

How you Put it Across

- Is there a clear structure – beginning, middle and end?
- Does your voice/body language convey interest/ passion/enthusiasm?
- Is your language appropriate to your audience – not too much jargon?
- Do you know your material well enough?
- How will you include the audience – e.g. by making good eye contact with all?
- Is the style varied enough to be interesting?

Technical Aids

- Are you familiar with the aids/equipment you are using?
- Can all visual aids be read easily?
- Have you considered how the presentation will look?
- How will you refer to notes without this being distracting?

You may want to add some prompts of your own if you know that there are some things about which you need to remind yourself. A good guide will be presentations you have witnessed in the past. What kinds of things have made it interesting for you, and what has been irritating or distracting?

If you are preparing a presentation in advance, it is helpful to practise by presenting it to someone who will give you an honest opinion as to how well it comes across. If you cannot do this, it is still a good idea to rehearse so that you are sure you are keeping within the time allowance. Assessment Centres are usually time-constrained and assessors may be very rigid about time! Even if you are preparing on the day, give yourself enough time to run through it quickly. As a general guide, it will take a little more time to present to an audience than it does when you are going through it on your own. Be prepared to take out some material if you are running out of time – just talking faster is seldom impressive! If you are clear in advance what you have to cover, and what is embellishment, it will be easier for you to be flexible "on the hoof".

Common Faults

Here is a list of some of the things that let people down when they are presenting. You may have other specific things that you know you are guilty of to add to the list:

- Failure to prepare for *that specific* audience.
- Talking too fast - or too slow. Either way you lose people.
- Over complicated or trying to cram too much in.
- Using jargon that is unfamiliar to the people you are presenting to.
- Too many words, no pictures or diagrams.
- Confusing visual aids - complex diagrams or distractions.
- Too general - not enough specific examples to bring it to life.
- Lack of structure - no route map.
- Dull tone of voice - not varied.
- Distracting mannerisms - jiggling coins or repeating an irrelevant phrase.
- Not including the audience - eye contact, questions.
- Being apologetic or tentative instead of using positive language.

If this seems a lot to remember, sift it down to the two or three things that will make your presentation better.

Graphology

Graphology is a form of assessment that uses an analysis of your handwriting. You are unlikely to come across this in the UK, USA or Australia but it is popular in some European countries - hence the reason for including it here. In a sense, it is used as an alternative to personality questionnaires. There is a debate about how useful this form of assessment is, and indeed a study carried out to measure its effectiveness found that it was no better than chance at predicting characteristics. This being the case, if you are asked to provide a handwriting sample to be assessed in this way, I would advise you to seek an opportunity of discussing the result as part of the assessment procedure. Then, if any judgments about you are being made that are out of line with the way you see yourself, you will have a chance to put the record straight!

Its effectiveness was no better than chance at predicting characteristics.

Guided Tour

You may be given the opportunity of a guided tour as part of the assessment day agenda. Strictly speaking, if you are being shown round the place where you would work if appointed, this is not part of the assessment. However, in practice, the people who show you round will inevitably make judgments about you and might make comments to the official assessors. So it is as well to make sure that you don't give a negative impression during this session. Of course, this also applies to informal discussion, perhaps over lunch, with other employees who are present but not actively assessing your capability.

Common sense should make you careful about expressing opinions in a sarcastic or critical way. There is no harm in being constructively critical, or in asking questions, but a degree of sensitivity is usually appreciated. For example, before making any critical comments, you should make sure you know why things are being done in that way and if there are any plans to change them. Negative comments about the company could be interpreted as meaning that you don't want to be part of their future, whereas showing interest and being polite will always go down well.

The value of these informal opportunities to you can be very great. They can provide you with real insight into how the company works, how people interact – whether very formally or in an informal and friendly manner. You can see areas that are new to you as well as those that are familiar. It can also stimulate thinking and suggest things you might want to ask about if you are given the opportunity, for instance in an interview.

Summary

After an explanation of what is meant by an "Assessment Centre" the chapter centred mainly on different kinds of group exercises as these are very common components of assessment events. As group exercises focus on how you work with other people, it is important to be aware of your behaviour generally, and to use this awareness to remind yourself what you should and should not do. Some tips for guidance are included, but as everyone is different you could benefit from thinking about your own characteristics - assisted by others who know you well if possible - and constructing your own do/don't list.

Any exercise where you are being watched closely can seem strange, but you are guided to try to forget that the observers are there. They will not want to distract you from the exercise, and neither will they expect you to talk directly to them.

Other typical Assessment Centre exercises are also covered. New approaches are being devised all the time, and as technology advances there are bound to be different kinds of exercises as well as variations on the ones we have covered. Hopefully the principles will stand you in good stead whatever the exercises are.

Chapter 8:

The Interview

Why are you being Interviewed?

It is very natural for employers to want to meet candidates personally. They are interested in the future well-being of the company and want to ensure that the people employed are going to add to its success and not damage it. Most of us think that we can get a "feel" for someone we meet and talk to. Even where it is likely that more objective selection methods are going to give a more accurate view of the match between the person and the job, the subjective feel of a face to face interview is valued. Of course, that "feel" can be obtained outside the formal environment of an interview, however, historically it has been a favoured method of selection, and is likely to remain so.

The question of why you are being interviewed is therefore not a straightforward one to answer. The anxiety about doing without it is probably a major factor in its being retained as a selection tool, rather than its utility. Most people are not as good at judging character as they would like to believe, but the idea of employing someone without first conducting an interview is seldom countenanced.

There are some things that are unique to you, and so will not be covered by standard tests or generic group exercises. The interview therefore has an important place in finding out about your experience and way of thinking about issues.

If you are interviewed by those with whom you will be working they might also be interested in the "chemistry" between you. In other words, they might want to satisfy themselves that you are someone with whom they would like to work. This should not, however, make you try to please them. Often managers will be looking for someone who can stimulate their thinking and challenge them, so if you always agree with them they might wonder if you would ever dare to put forward a different view. The best guidance here is to be true to yourself. Agree if you genuinely do, and disagree – politely – if you think differently.

The Development of the Interview

In the days when selection decisions were made largely on the basis of an interview, the possible biases that influenced the interviewer could have as much effect on the decision as anything the candidate said. There are many stories about interviewers who would never employ anyone with a limp handshake or who wore brown shoes. Some interviewers were proud, without much justification, of their ability to use their instincts to pick the right candidate. In reality, what they thought of as "instinct" was often a reflection of their own experience and prejudices.

More worryingly, it appeared from research that the actual decision was often made in the first moments of the interview. If they liked their first impression, the decision was likely to be favourable, although there was the possibility that the candidate could damage this perception as the interview progressed. It was much harder for a candidate to change an unfavourable impression, and even potentially effective individuals could be rejected with no valid reason. Because this was very much a subjective process, different interviewers could have different views of the same person, and success in being selected was influenced by who the interviewer was as well as by who the candidate was.

The unreliability of the interview as a selection tool was clearly a situation that could not be allowed to continue. Quite apart from the danger to the organisation of selecting people who were not effective, legislation was introduced to protect people from being discriminated against on the basis of their race or sex, and, in America, this extended to age also. This in turn generated pressure to ensure that interviewers received training so that they could conduct interviews that were fair and that focused on the qualities and characteristics required to be successful in the job. You should not therefore face intimate questions about your family life or whether you intend to have children!

That said, interviewers remain human with all the failings and subjectivity that being human entails. Being trained to avoid bias does not fully remove the possibility that decisions are made subjectively rather than objectively. However, it does reduce it dramatically. Taken alongside other selection tools, such as the ones described earlier in this book, selection is now much more fair to the candidate and much more accurate for the employing company.

There is another important reason for organisations retaining the interview, and this should be reassuring to candidates. One of the reasons they want to meet you personally is so that they can sell the company and the job to you. An impersonal process is less likely to make a good candidate choose to work for one organisation rather than another. It is useful to remember this when you are being interviewed as it will help you to regard it as a conversation rather than a "test" that you have to pass.

An Overview

The interview remains a potentially useful tool for exploring some issues that are more difficult to assess by other means. These include:

- **Motivation** - how committed you are to your work and how much effort you are prepared to put in.
- **Resilience** - your response to stress, problems and disappointments.
- **Aspirations** - where you see your career going and how this position fits in with your life plan.
- **Technical expertise** - your level of knowledge and how you keep yourself up to date with developments in your specialist field.

- **Loyalty** - the degree to which you will support the company and make a personal commitment to its success.

There are also some characteristics that might be demonstrated by your responses in a psychometric test or your participation in a group exercise, but can be further probed during an interview. Examples of these are:

- **Confidence** in your interactions with other people.
- **Communication skills** - how articulate you are and how good you are at listening.
- **Responsibility** - how far you take ownership of problems or objectives.
- **Impact** - how you come across generally, including your appearance and manner.

You may be interviewed by more than one person, either in sequence or together. In either case, it is likely that the different interviewers will have decided between them which areas they will cover. For instance, it is quite common to have someone from the Personnel or Human Resources Department covering areas relating to personal qualities, with the functional manager asking questions of a more technical nature.

Hopefully you have gone through Chapter 2 and the exercise suggested in Chapter 3, to think carefully about what qualities, characteristics and experience the employer is looking for. You will now be well-placed to review your personal as well as work history with a view to identifying evidence for each.

This chapter will cover the types of interview you are likely to come up against and will give you guidance to help you prepare to present yourself accurately and comprehensively to the interviewer.

As an aside, and an important one, you should be aware that employers are operating in a competitive market. They want to attract the best candidates, and are therefore as much selling to you as you are to them. Just as you want to give a good impression so that they will want to employ you, they want to attract you to the company and encourage you to accept the offer if they decide to make one. Knowing this is important because it sets the scene for a conversation in which both sides have an element of control.

The Unstructured Interview

Despite all the shortcomings of the more traditional form of interview, which can be thought of as the interviewer trying to get to know you without the assistance of a framework or structure, you might find that some companies have this as part of their selection procedure. The best that can be said of this is that it gives the opportunity for you and the interviewer to see if you can establish rapport. It also serves as a chance for the company to sell itself to you.

This kind of interview may well seem inefficient. The interviewer may spend much of the time reviewing information already supplied - your CV and application form for instance - in which case there is little added value in the exercise. It also suggests that the interviewer has not spent sufficient time preparing for the conversation, as the kinds of questions being asked don't reveal any new information. Clues that the interview is unstructured might be:

- The interviewer keeps referring back to your application form or CV.
- The conversation is more about the company than about you and your experience, or
- The conversation covers your experience generally rather than probing specific areas.
- The interviewer does a lot of talking.
- There are obvious "pet questions" - such as "Which historical figure do you most admire?" or "What would you do if you won a million pounds?".

You should not, however, think of it as a waste of time if you believe you are participating in an unstructured interview.

The onus is on you to ensure that you create opportunities to put forward the information you want the interviewer to know.

Given that this kind of interview may well subject you to unpredictable questions, of the type mentioned above, you might want to give some thought as to how you can respond. For instance, unless there is a figure from history who immediately comes to mind, you might be thrown by that question. Don't be! Instead try to imagine what lies behind the question – possibly the interviewer is interested in the qualities you admire in other people, so you could answer that question instead. ("No individual comes to mind immediately, but I can tell you generally what I admire in other people.") If you are completely stumped, you can always ask the interviewer what he or she wants to know about you, so that you can respond more easily. ("Nothing comes to mind – what would that tell you about me? Perhaps I can answer in a different way.")

The Structured Interview

One of the ways of helping interviewers to be as objective as possible in making their decision, whilst covering the required ground, is to have a structure. There are various different forms of the structured interview, but they share some common characteristics:

- The interviewers will have some specific things they want to find out. These may relate to experience or personal qualities, and they will probe the same areas for every candidate.
- The interview will follow a format, with a definite start, middle and end. You may therefore be discouraged from asking questions of your own until the appropriate point in the interview has been reached.

In some cases the structure will be very rigid, and the interviewers may follow a script in asking specific questions. However, a more conversational style, in which the interviewers merely keep track of what they need to cover and ask questions in a fairly natural way, is more usual.

The best interviewers will guide you skilfully through the interview, signalling when they want to move on to a different topic and summarising what they have heard so that you know you have got through to them. They will also be disciplined in only asking questions that relate directly to the qualities and experiences of interest for the job. However, most interviewers will bring more of their own personality to the task. They might not be so skilled at putting you at your ease, or they might have some "pet" questions they like to ask even though these are unnecessary.

There are many different kinds of structured interview. The next part of this chapter gives a picture of some that you might come across. These are:

- Biographical interview.
- Telephone interview.
- Competence based interview.

The Biographical Interview

A biographical interview is a form of structured interview where the content to be covered relates to your biography or life story. In essence, the interviewers are interested in finding out how far your background and experience relate to the criteria they have drawn up from profiling other people who have been successful in the past. Depending on the profile, the interest may include the type of school you attended, previous employers, your leisure activities and your experience aside from the specific job.

It is arguable that a biographical interview is likely to give preference to candidates who are similar to people already employed, and this is certainly the case sometimes. However, the profile could equally have been designed to do just the opposite, i.e. give preference to candidates who break the mould. You cannot change history – your biography – so you might also feel that this does not represent as fair a way of assessing your potential as other ways. Those who use the method would justify it in terms of probability – they choose to invest in people who are statistically more likely to succeed, even though this carries the risk of rejecting people who might be equally good, or even better, but who have different profiles.

The Telephone Interview

Although most interviews are face to face, you might be asked to participate in a telephone interview, usually as an early screening device before being invited to attend a further selection event. Typically a telephone interview will be conducted by an organisation that has been retained by the potential employer to assist in sifting candidates down to a short list.

Telephone interviews are often scripted and may be recorded so that the organisation conducting them has a way of ensuring quality control and also of comparing candidates' responses at leisure. Each question will probe a particular quality or type of experience that is required for successful performance. Scripting is a way of ensuring that the interview is fair – all candidates are faced with exactly the same questions. By conducting the interview without actually seeing you, many of the biases are removed – but of course not all. The interviewers can still detect your accent and other non-verbal information such as your tone of voice. Subjective judgments, based on how confident you sound or how quickly you respond to questions, may also be made. But by and large, this method is designed to be as fair and efficient as possible. Responses may be "scored" so that your overall total determines whether or not you are put forward to the next stage.

Being interviewed by telephone can be either more or less anxiety-provoking than face to face. You might find it strange because it is outside your experience. It can also be disconcerting not to have access to the reaction of the interviewers – just as they cannot see you, you cannot see them. If you are someone who is generally not comfortable using the telephone, this will add to your nervousness. As

Telephone interviews are often scripted.

with other exercises, it is hoped that by being prepared you will be able to counteract any of these negative feelings.

Of course, you might be very at ease using the telephone. This too can have its dangers, as you can easily slip into a more casual conversation. It would be a pity to waste the opportunity of selling yourself by being too chatty and failing to concentrate on the information that would take you on to the next stage in the selection procedure.

Apart from not seeing the interviewers, some people find it disconcerting that the flow of the conversation seems unnatural. As the interviewers will have a series of questions they have to ask, it may appear that they are changing the subject more frequently than you are used to in a less structured conversation. This is also the case in a face to face interview, but at least in that situation you have access to a wider range of cues to tell you that the interviewers are ready to move on to another topic – they might nod or turn pages or emphatically draw lines under their notes, or their facial expressions will let you know that they have covered the topic to their satisfaction.

The preparation guidelines for interviews generally will also apply here. You need to give some thought in advance to the experiences and personal qualities that you want to talk about. However, you have an advantage when the interviewers cannot see you. You will probably feel more comfortable having your notes to hand where you can refer to them while you are talking and listening. Keep these notes short! You don't want to be shuffling papers and spending time looking for long lists.

Additional things you will want to do in advance are:

- **Prepare the time** – the interview will be at a specific time, but it is up to you to make sure that it is a time when you can talk privately and without interruption. You might decide that it is best to do this when you are at home, in which case you may need to make arrangements that ensure you are not disturbed by other people who live there. If at work, you may need to alert other people to the fact that you are having a long telephone conversation and cannot be disturbed. Mental preparation helps too – decide in advance that you will not answer the doorbell or respond to the dog scratching at the door. Have a way of dealing with interruptions that you haven't managed to avoid – thinking about this in advance can make you less disconcerted by them when they happen.
- **Prepare the place** – you can decide where you are when you take the call. Make sure it is a place where you can sit comfortably and have everything you need

to hand. Remove things that will be in your way and that you will not need. It will be a long conversation, so if you need to have a glass of water available, get it in advance. You should have your CV and notes close to you where you can read them easily. Ideally, the pages should be spread out so that you can see each one without having to leaf through - use the walls if the desk is not sufficient. If you have a hands-free phone, this can be useful, but be aware that other noises in the room will also be detectable. A headset is preferable if you have access to one. You will also need a notepad to record any thoughts or ideas that come to you as you are listening to the question - and something reliable to write with!

- **Prepare yourself** - even though the interviewers cannot see you, you may find that you present yourself more effectively if you pretend that they can! Telephone sales people are often trained to smile when they are trying to sell, and to turn up at their desk looking smart and professional. You may of course choose to be interviewed wearing your dressing gown, but you might actually sound more convincing if you know that you look the part.
- **Remind yourself that the questions may not follow a natural flow**, and try not to be put off by this. If you feel that the interviewers are moving on too quickly and you have not said something important, say that there is something you'd like to add. Don't be afraid to ask for a question to be repeated. If necessary, check that you have understood the question by paraphrasing it back before you respond.
- **Check the general interview guidelines** - these also apply to telephone interviews.

The Competence based Interview

Competences (or "competencies") can be thought of as the behaviour that shows you have a set of underlying skills and knowledge. Many organisations will have a set of competences that they have drawn up to guide both recruitment and the on-going development of employees. In some cases there will be different sets of competences for different kinds of role, and there may also be different levels. At its most sophisticated, the company will have a matrix of competences - both different roles and different levels.

If you are being assessed against competences, you are being judged by the same criteria as existing employees. Of course, you may be one of those existing employees applying for a different job in your own company. However, if you are an external candidate, the chances are that you will only be selected if you do better than internal candidates.

Interviews that are based on competences will be structured, but skilled interviewers will use this structure flexibly to ensure they have probed adequately to assess the target competences.

Let us digress for a moment to look at what competences might be assessed by this method. Most sets of competences contain some items that are clearly related to business. Examples of Business Competences are:

- **Business sense** - having knowledge of the different business functions and how they inter-relate; using this knowledge to ensure all relevant parts of the business are involved in agreeing objectives and priorities.
- **Commercial awareness** - concentrating on activities that are central to increasing profit; having a clear commercial case for both increasing and decreasing costs.
- **Customer focus** - demonstrating an understanding of the customer perspective; basing decisions on customer data; giving priority to customer requirements.
- **External orientation** - keeping abreast of developments in the market; maintaining a useful network within the industry; assessing own results in terms of external benchmarks.

In addition to business competences, there will usually be a group of competences that cover interpersonal behaviour - how you behave when you are interacting with other people. Examples of Interpersonal Competences are:

- **Teamworking** - recognising and appreciating the strengths of others; being helpful and supportive of colleagues; building good working relationships.
- **Leadership** - giving direction to other people by negotiating objectives and priorities; developing talent; demonstrating an understanding of people's different motivations; making tough decisions where necessary.
- **Communication** - able to be easily understood both when communicating in speech and in writing; involving other people at the right time by informing and explaining; paying attention when listening to others; checking understanding.
- **Influencing** - able to put forward a convincing argument based on facts; using persuasive language; showing an understanding of others' requirements, doubts and concerns.

There might also be some competences that are more related to your personal characteristics and how these affect your behaviour. Examples of Individual Competences are:

- **Personal organisation** - effective at prioritising own work even when there are competing demands; maintaining a tidy workstation.
- **Drive** - showing energy and enthusiasm; being self-motivated and proactive in suggesting improvements.
- **Integrity** - being honest and trustworthy; treating people fairly and with respect.
- **Impact** - creating a positive impression by being smartly dressed and showing confidence; demonstrating a good grasp of the subject when presenting.

When you are being interviewed to assess some of these competences, the questions might probe different aspects of your life, not just your work experience, to establish whether or not you can show evidence. The interviewer may also want to be convinced that you use good judgment. For instance, you may be an excellent communicator, but wait too long before you decide to share your thoughts with other people, or you could have a huge amount of drive and not be sensitive to how this affects other people, or your customer focus might be so strong that you use your time responding to inappropriate demands.

Guidance on Handling Interviews

Very skilful interviewers will be aware that your real experience is a better guide than what you say you would do in theory, but you may find that you are asked questions of a more speculative nature. For instance, a good interview question might be: "How did you deal with a disagreement with your boss?" This would give the interviewers real data, whereas "What would you do if you disagreed with your boss?" only tells them what you think the right answer is! Your task is to ensure that you present yourself as accurately as you can whether or not the interviewers are very skilful.

If you are faced with a speculative question, you can choose how to respond. For instance, with the above example you could decide to respond as if the better question had been asked: "Can I tell you about a real example? I waited for a time when I could talk to her alone and explained that my analysis had come up with a different answer from hers. I asked her if I could talk her through it so that we could see together if I'd made a mistake. She was fine about it, but afterwards said she wished I'd spoken up sooner as the delay could have been costly. That encouraged me to be more ready to voice my doubts." An answer like that shows the interviewer not just what you have done in the past, but also what you have learnt from that experience.

Remember that you can also call on your experience outside work when responding to interviewers' questions. For instance, if they are looking for a candidate who is able to organise other people, and you have not yet had experience of managing a team at work, you might be able to think of occasions outside work that demonstrate this. For example: "One of my pastimes is fishing, and every so often we need to get a work party together to clear rubbish and weed from the ponds we use. I volunteered to take this on. I decided that it would be too time-consuming to contact everyone directly, so I worked out a system whereby each person I phoned would then phone three others. We had to make sure we had equipment too, so I got everyone to say what they could supply, regardless of whether or not they were going to be there in person. We often have a problem with turn-out so I thought of some incentives. It's a bit difficult without a budget, but we arranged to have a nice pub lunch and at the end we had a sort of awards ceremony – for the most unusual find, the person who got dirtiest and the most inventive use of rope."

The candidate in that example has demonstrated some important managerial characteristics. He did some planning ahead of time, involved other people, delegated responsibility and also addressed the need to motivate people.

Of course, there will be times when interviewers ask questions that are outside your experience. You might be able to anticipate this if you have a good idea of what they are looking for, and so again be able to prepare yourself. Let's say you are being interviewed about a position in an industry outside your experience. You might, for instance, have worked in clothing distribution, and are now applying for a position with an engineering firm that makes specialist tools. On the surface, there is very little overlap – the products and market are completely different.

In a situation like this, you might need to think more deeply about the underlying principles that you can apply in either environment. These might include:

- Being accurate in identifying requirements.
- Ensuring timely delivery.
- Getting people to co-operate to resolve problems.

- Checking that the resources are available to complete tasks.

However, it will not be enough to show that some of your experience has more general applicability. You will also need to have thought about how to fill the real gaps in your knowledge or experience. A response like "I'll spend the first three months trying to find out about the industry" is unlikely to impress! Filling the gaps might be by:

- Using your existing network to identify people who know more about the industry than you do.
- Talking to current customers about their experience – what problems do they have.
- Talking to suppliers – what is their view of the market.
- Reading the trade press to learn about topical issues.

You should never minimise aspects of your background that might be of concern to an employer. If you give the impression that you think you have little to learn, or that you have not grasped the difficulties you might face, you will come across as either arrogant or naive. It gives interviewers more comfort if you can show that you have given these issues serious thought and have come up with at least the start of a plan to make yourself effective in the shortest possible time. There's no harm in asking questions – maybe the interviewers have some suggestions that might help. However, if you haven't had any thoughts of your own, you are likely to leave the interviewers' concerns intact.

A general point is that many people think that they are reducing their chances of being selected by exposing a weakness or shortcoming. This is not necessarily the case. The people interviewing you inhabit the real world where:

- Nobody's perfect.
- People who are on top of a job on the day they start sometimes lose interest and leave.
- Even if you are competent in the job at the outset, the job is likely to change.

- Having insight into a weakness or limitation is better than being ignorant of it.

The way you respond to tricky questions is as important as the response you give. Imagine that the interviewers have told you about a problem they faced recently and asked you how you would have dealt with it. How would you feel about the following responses?

1. I wouldn't have a problem with that. I've dealt with lots of similar situations.
2. I haven't a clue – I've never heard of anything like that before.
3. When I had a similar situation, this is the way I tackled it.
4. It's outside my experience, but it sounds as though you needed to make a quick decision. I've certainly had to do that before.
5. You just go through the same process as before – analysis, diagnosis and action.
6. I think I'd handle it this way. But as it's new to me I'd want to check out my solution with a couple of people first if possible.

Before reading on, think about how each of these responses comes across to interviewers. Obviously there is no one right answer, but you might have come up with impressions like the ones below.

Responses 1, 3 and 5 suggest that you have an answer. There is a danger that the first response just makes you appear to be over-confident – arrogant. The interviewers might also feel patronised or belittled, which would not make them want to work with you. Response 3 is more tactful and balanced if you are familiar with that kind of problem. The fifth response makes it look as though you have a set way of dealing with any problem – which may in fact be the case, and you might have a lot of confidence in your methodology. However, it can also make you appear rigid, as if you always follow the same recipe.

Responses 2 and 4 might have been made by a candidate who didn't have an answer to the problem. Obviously response 2 seems a bit thin. It might be honest, but not impressive. Response 4 is a stronger and more positive reply, and might satisfy the interviewers if you convinced them that you were able to make decisions under pressure and that is what they were looking for. Response 6 is similarly honest about the situation being new to you, and you are also showing that you acknowledge that your solution may not be the right one because of that.

Guidelines when Preparing for your Interview

If you have been interviewed in the past, take some time to reflect on those experiences. What do you think you did both before and at the time that made you present yourself well? What kinds of things have let you down in the past? Take a moment to jot down some personal reminders about the things you want to make sure you carry on doing, and those you want to do differently.

What about other people you know who have been interviewed recently? Maybe they have some stories that will help you to think about your preparation.

You won't know in advance exactly what questions will be asked, but by being well prepared you are in a better position to answer any questions. Being prepared is also important to make you feel more confident on the day. Some things you could consider as part of your preparation are:

- Make sure you review your CV.
- Remind yourself of what the interviewers are likely to be looking for, and the areas of your experience that you can draw on.
- Practise saying positive things about yourself.
- Be honest about your experience gaps, and have a plan to address them.

General Reminders

Elsewhere in this book there is guidance about how to present yourself when you are a candidate. Your assessors may not be especially impressed by your turning up looking clean and smart, and looking as though you would fit in – that will be what they expect. However, they are likely to have a negative response if you have clearly made no effort or appear out of place.

Interacting with complete strangers for an hour or so can be tiring and stressful. Mental preparation will be helpful – being positive and realistic about yourself, showing empathy towards the interviewers, and making sure there are not other competing issues on your mind will all help.

As with any assessment exercise, the more you know about your own characteristics, the better able you will be to control and make positive use of them. Be alert to your signs of stress or discomfort – fidgeting, giggling, looking down, chewing your nails – so that you can control them at the time. Avoid language or mannerisms that will distract the interviewers from assessing you positively – swearing, winking, nose-picking are all out!

Another thing you might want to think about is how you can relax yourself at the time of the interview. If you can adopt a relaxed posture when you first sit down, this will help you throughout the interview. Sitting well back in the chair will give you better support than perching on the edge. Think: head up, shoulders down. This will automatically stop you from being hunched up and will move your arms slightly away from your body. Then think about your feet – we often tense these when under pressure, possibly in preparation for running away! Think: toes down so that your feet are not pointing upwards.

So, in addition to preparing for the content of the interview questions, you could also do some personal preparation:

- Take care over your personal presentation – looking clean, tidy and smart is expected, and "fitting in" is an advantage.

- Think about your own characteristics - the things you might want to control or avoid during an interview, and prepare yourself mentally.
- As you sit down for your interview, be aware of your posture and relax it - then you can forget about it afterwards.

Summary

This chapter has covered the background to modern interview techniques and given you an overview of the types of interview you are likely to encounter as a candidate. There is also some guidance about how to deal with your interview and how to prepare yourself in advance, and as you start being interviewed.

The "competences" you first met in Chapter 2 have been elaborated. You might now want to think further about how to articulate your own experiences so that you can demonstrate the competences of interest to your interviewer.

As well as the general guidance here, there may be points you have picked up from your own or others' experience that you want to bear in mind, and you are encouraged to remind yourself of these.

Chapter 9:

In-depth Individual Assessment

For some positions, it is not regarded as appropriate to ask candidates to attend an Assessment Centre. This might be because it is unlikely that a day can be found when the whole pool of candidates could attend, or because there is a sensitivity about candidates meeting each other. In these situations, your assessment will be an individual one. You may still be asked to do some of the things that have already been described – for instance, you will almost certainly be interviewed and you may also be asked to complete some psychometric tests or to produce a presentation.

If you are a candidate for a very senior position, or one that is extremely important to the success of the company, your potential employer might ask you to spend some time with an external consultant, often a professional psychologist, to provide another view of your capabilities or potential. Whereas your track record is an excellent indicator of how you are likely to perform in similar situations and environments, where there is substantial change it is often more important to look at how you are likely to handle new situations, how you learn and adapt.

The benefit of getting feedback has been raised previously. If you are asked to meet an external consultant, your session is likely to include at least some opportunity to get detailed feedback. Most professional consultants will ensure that you leave the session knowing, in outline at least, what they will be reporting to their client – the potential employer. The best ones will insist that you have an opportunity to review this information in detail, and will offer you a second session to discuss your profile and any development pointers that come out of it. In other words, recognising that your time is valuable, they will want to ensure that you get something out of the process whether or not you end up working for the client company. As this involves some additional expense for the employer, they are only likely to request this if you are already thought to be someone they want to employ. You should therefore see this as a positive sign.

Why an External Consultant?

You may wonder why the company has asked you to meet someone who is not part of their organisation. There are likely to be a variety of reasons, including at least some of the following:

- The consultant knows the company well and can provide an independent and objective assessment based on his or her knowledge of what is required in the future.
- The specialist, professional skills of the consultant, who will usually be a psychologist, in understanding people are beyond those of the other, internal assessors.
- Candidates will often reveal more to someone who they know will treat personal information confidentially, and who can also help them personally.
- The consultant will provide either confirmation of the company's assessment or will highlight additional points that the company might miss – these might be warning signs, or could be additional potential that has not previously been recognised.
- The company may be confident in their choice of candidate, but require more explicit guidance on how to support and develop this individual to ensure he or she can be as successful as possible.
- The company may be confident in their choice of an external candidate, but want to have assurance that they are getting someone who can add more to the role

than existing employees – it is often difficult to compare people who have different kinds of experience.
- The consultant has experience of a wide range of organisations and can therefore assist by "benchmarking" the candidate against high performers in other companies.
- The organisation wants to ensure standards are consistent across different divisions or across different subsidiary companies, and therefore has a policy of using a specialist adviser to assist in making selection decisions.
- There may be doubts about the capability of someone who is relatively young or inexperienced, and where the assessment of potential is more important than track record.
- Technical capability is known to be strong, but the ability of the candidate to influence, lead change or deal with new stresses (such as taking up an appointment in another country) needs to be explored.

The external consultant is not the decision-maker, but will be able to assist in ensuring the right decision is made. In some cases this means ensuring that the decision made can work – by highlighting what the company needs to do to help the person they select to be effective.

The Process of an In-depth Individual Assessment

As this assessment is undertaken by someone outside the company you are applying to, you may be asked to go to the consultant's office rather than that of the company. Most in-depth assessments will contain two elements:

- An interview.
- Psychometric tests.

They might also contain other exercises similar to the ones covered in Chapter 7, Assessment Centres, although of course you will not be involved in a group exercise as you are being assessed on your own. Any additional exercises are likely to be case studies or simulations, so that you have the opportunity of demonstrating some specific performance that the consultant can discuss with you.

The interview may be the main part of the process, in which case it is likely to be quite lengthy and wide-ranging, and might also include discussion of the other parts of the assessment. Depending on the methods used by the consultant, the session can take between half a day and a full day. Where a review of the profiles from tests or your performance doing other exercises is included, your response to this may also form part of the assessment. (If you are invited to return for a second session to review the judgments made about you, this will not form part of the assessment, and in any case the decision is likely to have been made by this time.)

Consultants should explain to you how they will report back to their clients. In particular, they should let you know what kind of information is not disclosed. It is usually the case that much of the content of your discussion can remain confidential and it is the judgment, not the account of specific incidents, that is passed on to the client. If you are in any doubt, you should ask for this to be clarified. You might feel more comfortable talking about a previous employer, mentioning sensitive information or disclosing what you consider to be intimate details of your personal history if you know that the consultant will respect that confidentiality.

In the ideal world, the consultant will be sufficiently skilled and confident in his or her judgments to share any hypotheses with you, so that it is a process in which both of you genuinely participate. You would leave the session knowing in broad terms what was going to be said or written about you and would have had the opportunity of putting right any misconceptions.

There are some consultants who rely solely on tests and exercises without interviews. If you are asked to participate in an assessment of this kind, my guidance would be to try to negotiate an opportunity to discuss the findings before

"I promise I won't tell them about your stamp collection."

. . . disclosing what you consider to be intimate details of your personal history.

they are passed on or, if this is not possible, with one of the decision-makers in the company subsequently. You want to be sure that any judgments made about you are accurate, and also to have the chance to show that you are aware of your weaknesses and can address them. If the company is resistant to this reasonable request, you might wonder what they would be like to work for!

What does "In-depth" mean?

The consultant adds value to the process by helping the employing company to make predictions about how the successful candidate is likely to perform and how he or she can learn and develop. In order to do this, the consultant will want to elicit from you the kinds of enduring themes and patterns in your behaviour that are likely to be repeated. It is not just *what* you are capable of doing, but also *how* you are most likely to go about it. The way you approach things will be influenced by many factors, and the consultant's job is to help you to reveal what the important factors are.

As an example, the consultant might be interested in how you make decisions. There are many different approaches to decision-making, and no single approach is better than another. All have their inherent strengths and weaknesses. In exploring how you make decisions, the consultant is not judging whether your process is a good one or not, but rather is trying to describe it accurately. This is different from the assessment of how good your decisions are. By separating the two elements - describing how you go about it and determining how effective you are - the consultant can work out what would be the right kind of development for you, as opposed to for someone who has a different style or approach.

If we take this example further, we could see that people make their decisions in different ways. Let's take a situation where someone is about to buy a new car. How might different people go about making the decision as to which car to choose? For instance:

- **Using intuition** as a starting point - getting a "feel" for what the best option is likely to be and then testing it out. Such people might have a sense of the kind of car they would like to drive and select cars to test on that basis. They would "just know" when they found the right one, and might be prepared to compromise on some features to proceed with that decision.
- **Using experience and data** to identify problem areas and concentrating on the variables that are most out of line. These people might think about the things that they don't like in their current cars, and check out with other people what problems or concerns they have about theirs. They would rule out cars that could not address the major concerns even if they were excellent in other ways.

- **Using research and analysis** in a structured way. Here people might start by looking broadly at the pros and cons of different models and draw up short lists representing criteria or principles that mattered to them – for instance, best value together with good fuel consumption. Depending on the criteria, they might get to a stage where they had a single "right" answer.
- **Using pragmatism** and being realistic about what is possible. The budget, size of garage, need for large boot and child-proof locks might be the starting point for these people. They might be prepared to go with a car they didn't like the look of once they had found one that met their basic needs rather than spend time searching for an even better solution.
- **Using trusted advisers** and experts to guide the decision. These people might talk to people who know a lot about cars to get advice as to which models to consider. They might be strongly influenced by experts who counselled against a particular manufacturer. They might even effectively delegate the decision to someone else having explained their requirements. They would feel satisfied with their choice, and recognise that this had saved them a lot of time and effort.

You might think that most people would use some combination of approaches rather than just one approach, and of course this is what happens in reality. However, most people will have a preference for one or two styles of decision-making, and will return to them when making different kinds of decisions. Their attitude to risk will also be relevant – some people are more prepared to take a chance when the wrong decision has major resource implications, whereas others would be more cautious and want to be certain before closing on their decision.

You can probably see from even this one example that it is not straightforward to get a good picture of an individual's predominant style. This is why the consultant is likely to ask questions about many different aspects of your life – how you were brought up and what you spend your time on when you have free choice as well as what you do at work.

The sources of information that help the consultants make the assessment will often go beyond what you would expect in a more conventional selection interview. However, they are not making a judgment about the nature of your experience or background. For instance, if you do not have a university degree, this will not be viewed either positively or negatively. What will be of interest, however, will be whether you considered this option and what led you to decide to take a different route.

Depth is therefore partly concerned with how far into your background and experience the consultant asks you to go, and also the degree of probing into individual incidents and experiences. There might be an event that appears to be given more attention by the consultant than you gave it at the time. This will be because the consultant has found a "rich vein" that helps build a good picture of the sort of person you are.

How to Approach an In-depth Assessment

There is very little work to do in preparing for this kind of assessment. If you are not sure exactly what form the assessment will take, for instance whether tests will be involved, and how long it is likely to last, you might want to ask some questions to clarify this. Bear in mind that the location may not be the same as the one you attended for an interview with the company.

When you meet the consultant, there may be some questions you have about the boundaries of confidentiality or how you will get feedback from the process. It might be worth making a note of anything you want to cover so that if it has not been addressed you can raise it with the consultant.

The main thing you should think about is your mental preparation. Some people welcome the opportunity to spend time talking about themselves and exploring their experience in a way they seldom - if ever - make time for. Others might find the process intrusive or tiring. Hopefully you will view the experience positively and try to ensure that you get something out of it for yourself, whether or not you are successful in your job application. If you are to do this, it helps to be open and honest with the consultant. If something is preventing you from being completely open on a certain topic, it is worth explaining this rather than just being cagey. The consultant should be sensitive to things you would rather not discuss, for whatever reason. On the other hand, you should remember that the session is part of a selection process and not try to railroad it for personal counselling either!

Summary

If you are asked to undergo an in-depth individual assessment, take it as a compliment! The company is interested in you and prepared to spend additional money finding out more about you. As this is often a more personal assessment, you can also regard it as an opportunity to find out more about yourself and to work with an expert to uncover what makes you successful and where you could improve further.

For many people this will be a new experience and the consultant will understand if you have questions about the process and how information will be used.

If you are given an opportunity to review the information subsequently, you are encouraged to make use of this as a way of increasing self-awareness and exploring how you can develop yourself further.

Chapter 10:

Doing Your Best

We have reached the stage at which you are getting ready to present yourself to your prospective employer. If you've followed the advice of the previous part of the book you will have thought about your own requirements and done what you can to find out how far the organisation is likely to meet them. This means that if you have decided to go ahead and attend the selection event, you are doing so with enthusiasm. You will have investigated the company as well as you can, so that you know not just about the role you'd be expected to play, but also what kind of competences or qualities they will find attractive. The experiences and talents you have that they are looking for will be familiar to you, and you will have trawled your own background to think of examples you can use to show how well you will meet their needs. You will also have evaluated yourself objectively so that, where you fall short of the requirements, you have thought about how you could close the gap.

This all represents information that helps you to sell yourself to prospective employers, to demonstrate how you can be of use to them and how motivated you are to work for them. Hopefully you'll also know what to expect of the assessment process too, so that nothing will be too much of a surprise. You may also have prepared a set of questions you want to raise with them.

It is now time to ask yourself how you are feeling when you anticipate attending the selection event; what other preparation will help you to present yourself effectively? Are you nervous or confident – or a bit of both? Most employers will make some allowance for the natural nervousness a lot of people have when they are under scrutiny, but it is still down to you to show them what you've got. Are you perhaps so confident that you could be fooling yourself into thinking you don't have to do anything other than turn up?! How can you make sure that you are mentally prepared to do your best?

Getting Ready to do Well

Recognising the Signs

What do you already know about yourself in similar situations - other job assessments, interviews, times when you've had meetings that have caused you anxiety, tests and examinations? Most people will have a lot of experience to draw on, for example: driving test, meeting partner's parents for the first time, presentations, being summoned to the headteacher's office, hospital appointments. Think broadly about any situation you have experienced that has similar elements - where you have been under scrutiny. There are probably some things that happen to you time after time, things that you can predict you will think or feel when faced with a stressful situation.

Some of these will be familiar responses that you have *in anticipation* of the stressful event, whilst others will happen *during* the event. These might include:

- Not sleeping well the night before.
- Butterflies in the stomach.
- A sense of excitement.
- A sense of dread.
- Going over and over things in your head.
- Finding it hard to concentrate or attend to what people are saying to you.
- Getting stomach pains or headaches.
- Sweaty palms.
- Being more alert than usual.

- Moving paper around rather than achieving anything.
- Eating comfort food.
- Going further into your shell.
- Biting your nails.
- Feeling on top of the world - powerful and optimistic.
- Being irritable with other people.
- Being more accident prone than usual.
- Talking a lot.
- High pulse rate - perhaps being more aware of your heart beating.

You will recognise these as being common signs of stress, some positive responses to the adrenalin in your system and others less positive. It is not a surprise if you might be aware of some of these before attending a selection event. However, this is not an exhaustive list. There are many ways of experiencing stress, both the positive and energising feelings we get when we are stimulated, and the negative side when things are getting on top of us. You might already know what your personal response is likely to be. Other people who know you well might be able to add to the picture.

Make a list of as many of these as you can think of, and then try to remember how you responded when you were in the situation.

- What was good about the way you presented yourself?
- What happened to make you feel better, more confident, less anxious?
- What factors contributed to your doing well?
- What was not so good?
- How did your thoughts and feelings get in the way of your achieving the best result?
- How could you have improved the way those occasions went?

By doing this you are building up a picture of how you typically respond to demanding situations, and what kinds of things make it better or worse.

Feeling in Control

When reflecting on how we have performed in the past, it is often easier to blame things around us than see clearly what we could have done differently. We can say it was circumstances or other people, and forget that we often have an influence on how things turn out. One of the characteristics of people we might describe as being more successful is that they believe they are generally powerful and can influence what happens to them rather than feeling powerless. They operate in the same world as everyone else, but they think about things in a way that makes them feel more in control.

Changing the way we feel about something we anticipate as likely to be stressful can be very helpful. You might think it is difficult to change our feelings, but if you think back you will probably be able to identify times in the past when your feelings have changed. Perhaps there's a food or drink you used to hate that now you like. Maybe you once wanted an individual to be your friend, but now you are not interested in him. There might be an activity you feared, but now take part in confidently. Or you once used to prefer a certain kind of music, and your tastes have altered. All these are examples of feelings changing.

Example 1

"When I took my driving test I was really nervous, but I also felt well prepared. I knew what to expect and lots of people had given me advice about how to handle it – like make sure when you look in the mirror it's obvious to the examiner that you're doing it. Anyway, in the first couple of minutes I made what I thought was a real hash of it – I started moving off without releasing the handbrake, then I stalled. I was so sure that I'd failed that after that I wasn't nervous any more – it was as if it didn't matter, so I relaxed and just got on with it. Everything else went fine and I passed."

This is a common example of being so anxious about the outcome that you do things wrong! However, it also gives a pointer as to how to make it go better. In this case, the thing that helped was to stop worrying about the end result and to concentrate on what was happening at the moment. The driver was able to relax once this was out of the way, and just treated the rest of the driving test as an ordinary event rather than something special.

A slight digression: there is another useful tip here that was recalled by this driver – to make sure that the examiner could see that he was doing the right things! This is also relevant when you are being assessed for a job. The people assessing you need evidence that you are able to perform as required – what evidence do you want to give them, either from previous work or activities outside work?

Addressing your Anxieties

Coming back to the main theme – how to make sure you are in a frame of mind that lets you put anxieties aside and concentrate on the here and now – how can you help yourself to do this before you start?

Some people find it helpful to indulge their "disaster fantasies" – to think about the very worst thing that could happen. Most of these will be so unlikely that by voicing them or writing them down they are able to put them into perspective. Our worst fears are usually the ones we haven't previously put into words, and when we finally articulate them they lose their power because we can see that they are irrational or extremely unlikely. Some of these disaster fantasies might seem more possible, but by thinking about them in advance, when you are not anxious, you can also start to think about how you would deal with the situation at the time and so make it less of a problem.

We can think of our anxieties as a helpful prompt. They can serve to highlight the areas where we need to concentrate in our preparation. There's little point in spending time rehearsing the things you are already confident about if this means you are neglecting the things that are likely to make you most nervous.

Example 2

"I put a suggestion into the staff suggestion box. The company had a problem with stuff being stolen by employees, and I thought stealing was made easier by having lockers where they could hide things until they went home. So my idea was to replace the locker doors with something you could see through. A week or so later I was asked to go and talk to my boss's boss to explain. I'd seen this guy a couple of times, but never actually spoken to him. When I went to see him I was really tongue tied. I just answered his questions with odd words, and I think I left him with the impression I hadn't thought it through – but I had! Afterwards I talked to some mates and they all thought it was a great idea and encouraged me to ask to see him again. The second meeting was much better – talking it through with my mates was like a practice session, and I knew what I wanted to say."

This illustrates the difference between *knowing* something and *conveying* it – being able to put it into words that other people understand and find interesting. This person learnt the hard way that it is helpful to talk things through first with people who are not judging you or what you have to say. In a more familiar and informal conversation, with supportive friends, the words came more easily.

This type of rehearsal can be engineered before going to a job interview or assessment. You already know what you want to say; now find some people who will help you rehearse – not to the point that you learn the exact words you will say, but enough to convey the ideas you want to get across. For instance, you could think of some examples that demonstrate your strengths and practise telling your friends about them.

Rehearsal also gives you the opportunity to get feedback "If we could see ourselves as others see us . . ." How did you come across? Were you using jargon that some people might not understand? Were you speaking loudly enough – or too loudly? Did you look comfortable, sound convincing, stick to the facts? Did you pitch it right - not too modest, but not too self-satisfied? People who know you and want to help you will often give you helpful feedback and advice about how you present the information you want to convey.

Recognising Faults

Getting feedback is a good way of learning about the areas we are already good at, and where we need to improve. By being honest about our faults we can start to reduce them. Maybe when you read on you will find some faults that sound familiar . . .

Example 3

"I thought I'd done well at the interview. I felt good about the job and thought there was a good rapport with the interviewer. So I was really disappointed when they told me I hadn't got it. Actually, I was a bit angry too – I didn't know what I could have done better. I decided to phone to find out how come they didn't want me. I was glad I did in the end, although it was quite painful in a way. They told me I hadn't really answered the interviewer's questions. It was as if I'd decided what I wanted to say, and wasn't really listening."

This person got useful feedback, albeit not pleasant. He'd gone all out to sell himself, but failed to address the issues that interested the interviewer.

Do you always listen when someone asks you a question? If you're not sure what is wanted, do you try to clarify it first? Do you take time to think of a response that really addresses what is of interest, or do you jump in too quickly?

Maybe you've had a similar experience in doing exams, when you've written a good essay, but not answered the question. Or perhaps you've been responding to someone's question only to get the response, "Yes I know all that, but . . ." If you know this is a potential failing, how can you guard against doing it when you go for your assessment? Sometimes the problem is being distracted by what you want to say or write, so that you're not really thinking carefully about the question.

If you are concentrating too much on what's in your head, it's hard to give your full attention. This may appear to contradict what has already been said about being prepared, but it doesn't really. Listening is a skill, and you can prepare yourself to listen carefully. It is acceptable to take a few moments to think after you've been asked a question, and that allows you to make good use of your preparation. If you have doubts about what the interviewer wants, you can always ask!

For example, "Why did you tell Mr Smith he was wrong?" is potentially ambiguous. The question could be about what you thought was wrong with what Mr Smith was doing, or about why you decided it was a good idea to tell him. "Do you want to know why I thought Mr Smith was wrong?" - This gives the interviewer the chance to re-tune your answer. "I'm more interested in why you thought you should tell him he was wrong."

Of course, if the question is written down, as it might be in a written exercise, such as in an "in-tray" exercise or psychometric test, you don't have the opportunity to seek clarification. A good written exercise will not be that ambiguous, so the important thing is to read it carefully and then read it again. Many people jump to conclusions. For example, if you see the number series 2..4..6..8..(?), you might quickly think that the answer is 10. But on re-reading the question you could find that you were asked for the next but one in the series, not the next one.

Another common fault is to assume that what you know is common knowledge, or that your skills are nothing special.

Example 4

"It's not that I lack confidence, it's just that I didn't think my committee experience was anything special. It didn't

occur to me that anyone would be interested in hearing about it. I suppose I think that if I can do it, so can everyone else."

There will be a range of things you have done that other people generally do not do – either they lack the skill or motivation, or they have not created the opportunity. It is possible that one or more of these will show evidence that is interesting to the people assessing you. If you fail to mention it, or talk about it in terms that make it seem trivial, you are not showing yourself to best advantage.

Sometimes drawing on other people's experience if you have none of your own to offer can be helpful – for instance, if you admire what someone else has done or aspire to a level of skill that you know someone else has achieved, this demonstrates that you know what "good" looks like.

Example 5

"I was going for a job where I would have to manage a small team. I'd never done that before, and I knew I was bound to get questions about it. What I did was to think about all the managers I could remember, what they did that I thought was good and what I hadn't liked. Then I asked a couple of people what they could remember about their first experience of being in charge of other people. When I got to the interview I was able to explain not only how I thought I would approach it, but also why on the basis of what I'd seen and heard."

Finally, there's a fine line between making sure you portray your strengths and over-selling yourself. When you are being assessed you can afford to put your modesty aside. However, skilled interviewers and observers will not be impressed if they doubt your integrity, so stick to the truth. Don't pretend that you are better at something than you actually are.

Summary

"Doing your best" means being in the right frame of mind to show what you can do and responding as well as you can to what you are asked during the assessment. There are some pointers as to the kinds of feelings and signs you may have that tell you when you are under pressure. Being aware of these helps to think about how you can overcome some of the negative effects of stress, the things that can get in the way of presenting yourself effectively. Knowing your faults (the things you tend to do over and over again) is helpful. Some frequently encountered faults which relate to selection are covered.

Preparation beforehand is a great help, but once you are in the situation you also need to make sure you are really listening or reading questions carefully.

Prepare by:

- Thinking of your own experience when under scrutiny.
- Confronting your fears and anxieties - say them, write them down.
- Acknowledging your faults so that you can address them.
- Rehearsing with friends who can help you to improve.

And, remember other tips elsewhere in this book, including:

- Deciding what to wear.
- Controlling distracting mannerisms.
- Practising a relaxed posture.
- Getting feedback to help you focus your preparation.
- Reviewing the information about yourself - your CV - rehearsing evidence and linking this to the Seven Signs of Success.
- Reviewing the information about the company and the competences likely to be assessed.

When in the situation:

- Listen carefully – don't be distracted by what's in your head.
- Don't be afraid to ask for clarification or to take time to think of a response.
- Read carefully – avoid jumping to conclusions.
- Draw on all your experience, direct and indirect.
- Value your experience objectively – don't under- or over-estimate it.
- Be in the present rather than worrying about the outcome.

Chapter 11:

When It All Seems To Be Going Wrong . . .

If you're reading this chapter, perhaps you have been applying for jobs for some time and finding that you keep being unsuccessful. Maybe you get short-listed sometimes, but always end up not being selected. This experience can damage your self-esteem so you might be feeling quite low and the prospect of going to yet another interview seems like an ordeal. You might be questioning your ability and even starting to think that you don't have anything to offer that employers value.

Are you really going for the Right Jobs?

At these times it is important to take stock and be realistic. If you have taken the advice in this book, you won't be wasting your time going for the wrong job – but it's worth checking your self-assessment and asking yourself if you are setting your sights too high. There are a number of possibilities you should consider:

- Even though you used to work in a job with a title similar to the ones you are applying for, are your *current* skills attractive to an employer?
- Do you find yourself competing against younger candidates, so that the salary you expect is higher than the company needs to pay to fill the position?
- Are you being realistic about your previous achievements – not just what you did, but how effective you were?

- Have there been technological changes that make your experience out of date?
- If you are seeking progression, are you being realistic about the size of the jobs you are going for, bearing in mind that you will have to learn about a new organisation?
- Are you applying for positions that attract many other people? Does the employer have the luxury of picking the "best" from a good field?

Some comments from others in your position might be helpful here:

"I know I can do the jobs I'm applying for, but so can a lot of other people. At first I kept bumping into the same people at Assessment Centres. A few of us kept in touch, and I found it discouraging that some of them got jobs before I did. Then I thought about it again, and decided that if they were so good I'd have more of a chance after they got jobs!"

"The job I'm about to start is smaller than the one I left. I'm ambitious, and I had to swallow a bit of pride in taking it. The thing was, I'd hit a ceiling in my last job – I could see that I wasn't going to get promoted. So I decided that I needed to find a company where I'd have more opportunities, even if it meant taking a backwards step initially. I think I'll be able to impress them more easily because I'm starting out doing something that's familiar, and where I can make some quick improvements."

"I'd been with the same company most of my working life when I was made redundant. I'd never really given much thought to how technologically advanced they were compared to other companies, but when I started applying for other positions I realised that we'd been behind the times. I had no experience of a lot of things I was expected to know, and so of course kept getting rejections. I spent some of my redundancy pay on re-training, and decided to take some contract work to get experience in different environments."

"In my late 40s, I was beginning to wonder if I'd ever get another job at the right level. I was existing on short-term contracts for a long time before this opportunity came up. At first I didn't look beyond the industry I'm familiar with, but when I started being more open-minded I found that I had some skills that transferred well into other environments."

"At the end of the day, it's a numbers game. You have to treat job hunting as a job in itself. People are moving companies much more these days, so there's bound to be more competition. If I'd been told I was unsuitable it would have made me think long and hard, but getting feedback that I did well at assessment, but someone else did better, gave me confidence to keep trying."

"I think I'm at a disadvantage because I have been out of work for a long time – over a year. Employers are bound to wonder what's wrong with you if no-one else wants to employ you! In the end, I decided to cast the net wider – and perhaps take a job I didn't really want, just so that I could start applying again in a year or so from a better base. I'm taking a long-term view and hoping that things will work out better in the future."

Your exercise in taking stock can be constructive, even if at first you feel disappointed and bruised by your experience of rejection. Maybe all the signs are that you are applying for the right kinds of jobs, but that you've been unlucky. If so, it's probably only a matter of time.

What if you have some doubts? How can you find out if you're chasing a wild goose?

The most obvious way is to get feedback from the companies that have rejected you. Some will be prepared to talk things through with you – as long as they don't think you're trying to blame them for the decision! Most people will be sympathetic if you say you want to learn from the experience and they will try to help you.

If you end up thinking that you are targeting the wrong

jobs, the obvious thing is to re-think your strategy in applying. This might mean:

- Targeting different kinds of companies or organisations.
- Applying for jobs at a different level.
- Basing your application on different skills – for instance, your technical rather than management skills.
- Working to improve your skills or experience perhaps by training or doing work for voluntary organisations.
- Being more flexible about salary, benefits, location or work patterns – for instance, accepting that you might have to travel or set up an office at home.

You are going for the Right Job!
The Application

Of course, you might be going for the right jobs, but still keep getting rejected. This book has concentrated on the selection procedure after your initial application has won you an invitation to the next stage, so one question might be: "Are you being invited sufficiently often, or does your application need attention?"

Fashions change in CVs and application forms. It isn't the intention to go into a lot of detail about applications – and if you are not sure that yours is good enough you should get advice from one of the many publications available on this subject, and from other people. However, here are a few ideas to be going on with:

- Some companies are now using the internet as a vehicle for applications, so it is important to have a CV that can easily be pasted.
- Handwritten applications MUST be legible and sufficiently clear to allow photocopying.
- Always do a draft first so that you know how much space you need, and use continuation sheets rather than trying to squash it into a space that's too small.

- Remember that whilst writing in capitals may look neater, it's actually harder to read - typing is better, or neat natural handwriting.
- Think about the language you use - make it positive, succinct and interesting.
- Explain gaps in employment - briefly.

Explain gaps in employment briefly.

- Achievements are more arresting than experience. (You might have been responsible for a four million pound budget, but not managed it very well.)

The Selection Process

If you're satisfied that your application is getting you a reasonable number of invitations to take the conversation further, perhaps you are not doing well enough when you go through the selection process.

"I never do well at numerical tests. I'm not too bad with figures in the 'real world' but it certainly isn't a strength, and at least there I'm not under time pressure. A couple of times I said at an Assessment Centre that I knew I'd score badly, and they re-assured me that it was only a small part of the decision. I didn't get the job in either case. Even if it's a small part of the decision, it means I have to be extra good to be considered. I've started asking about the assessment procedure in advance and if it involves a numerical test I don't go."

"Working in groups is very familiar to me. We're organised in project teams, and I spend a lot of my time sorting out problems with other people. I thought I'd be good in group exercises, but I found that with people I don't know – the other candidates – I get tongue tied. My friends were surprised, but they don't see me with strangers. I'm sure it has let me down."

"I get really nervous in interviews. I had some feedback from an interview – I wasn't successful needless to say – that I'd been shouting! Apparently my voice gets louder when I'm nervous. It was really helpful having someone tell me that."

"There was a selection day I remember when I just gave up. Chatting to the other candidates, I felt they all had more experience than I had, they were older and more confident. It made me stop trying – I was convinced I didn't have a chance. I could have kicked myself afterwards. The person who phoned to tell me I hadn't got the job said they really wanted to bring in someone with a fresh view, and if only I'd been more positive they would have loved to give me the chance."

"The job I was going for was in my own company. I was really resentful – I thought they should know what I was capable of because I'd worked there for a long time. Instead of thinking how I could sell myself, I kept referring to my track record. At the end, I was told that they knew all that. They wanted to know if there was anything else that would suggest I had further potential."

Presenting yourself well is part preparation, part attitude. Hopefully you'll have some pointers about how to make sure you prepare well from other parts of this book. But your attitude is also important. There's really no point in turning up for an interview or selection event unless you are determined to give it your best shot no matter what.

It's easy to be discouraged by other candidates, by poor interviewers or what you might think of as pointless exercises. Don't be discouraged! The company wouldn't waste time by considering you if you were not in with as good a chance as anyone else. Keeping up your motivation can be difficult, but, as you can see from some of the comments made by candidates, it is worthwhile because you need to think positively to show yourself positively. Keep your motivation up and your attitude positive by:

- Talking to yourself – quietly of course – and reminding yourself of your good qualities.
- Rehearsing the achievements you have had in the past.
- Thinking about the people who value your opinion, like you or respect your abilities.
- Letting other people help you – ask for advice and support.
- Consciously putting negative thoughts aside – if you find yourself thinking everyone's better than you, add that it's only in some things, and you're better than them in other ways.
- Remembering that a good Assessment Centre can find out things about you that you may not know about yourself – and these are also things that the company is looking for.

- Deciding that you'll enjoy the experience no matter what, and even if this time it doesn't work out, you'll have learnt something.

That's all very well at the time, but if you have had feedback that tells you there are specific areas where you fell down, you might also want to think of ways of improving your performance for next time. The following might help you both to diagnose and address the problem areas:

- Consolidate the feedback you have had from people who know you and from selection events.
- Identify specific parts of the process that need attention – is it preparation? Rehearsal? Performance in particular types of exercise – which ones?
- Go back to the previous chapters and find the parts that relate to your areas of weakness, and select the tips that are most relevant to your situation.
- Use your imagination to help you get a picture of what good performance looks like in the areas where you have not done well in the past, and make this picture your goal.
- Call on advice to assist you in developing an action plan, a set of activities that will help you to improve.

Networking – to Increase Opportunities

Maybe you are going for the right kinds of jobs, and your technique is not the problem. The difficulty might be that you are not finding sufficient opportunities to apply for positions.

A book on the subject of getting a new job would be incomplete without a section on networking. Of course I have already mentioned networking when thinking about how to find out more about the company, and as an aside noted that this is also useful to find out about positions you may otherwise have missed. Remember, your "network" is the group of people you are in contact with. When we talk about networking, we mean making use of your network - and perhaps enhancing it - to open up opportunities.

Even if you are actively job hunting, there will be some advertisements you will miss. Many jobs are filled without being advertised, and many candidates are invited to selection events because someone knows them rather than because they have answered an advertisement or been recommended by an agency. The more people you know who are likely to hear about positions that would interest you, the more likely you are to be approached or informed when something comes up.

A group of people you may want in your network are search consultants - "head hunters" - who are involved in recruiting people like you. A word of caution: Remember that "he who pays the piper . . .". Search consultants earn their fees from their clients, and will therefore spend most of their time being very focused on delivering what the client wants, rather than what you want. It will be hard for you to catch their attention by opportunistic contact - although if you are very lucky this might coincide with an assignment they are working on. Instead, think of how you can make use of the times when they want to talk to you, when they have initiated the contact. You are more likely to stay on their radar if you develop a rapport with them without making a nuisance of yourself!

If you are known before you attend a selection event, this can give you an advantage. Don't think of this as an unfair advantage - you could be known and ruled out without being invited to apply or be interviewed. The advantage if you are invited is that you know you have been considered and that someone thinks it is worth proceeding. This should give you further confidence.

If you do not already have a useful network, a word of warning. It takes time to build up your network and you need to think of it as a long-term investment. A search consultant estimated that it takes two years, so you may not benefit from your efforts immediately. However, don't assume that you have no network to start with. Go back to Chapter 3 which suggested how to make a start. Write down the names of everyone you know – each person you make a note of can potentially trigger another thought, someone you had forgotten about. (You can leave out children, but bear in mind that their parents might be good contacts.)

Add to this list from time to time – you will probably find that it's hard to think of everyone you know in one go. The "mind mapping" technique can be helpful here. Include the people you met on holiday and have since kept in touch with at Christmas. Include the list of people at the recent course you attended. Don't forget your friends and relations. Once you have a list to start with, each name is a potential contact with a new person.

Summary

There can be many reasons for not getting the job you want. Perhaps you are not applying for the right positions, or not finding out about enough opportunities. Your application might not be sufficiently attractive. Maybe you have not been realistic in evaluating yourself against the requirements of the job – your skills, experience or personal characteristics might not be a good fit.

Naturally you will be disappointed. However, there are things you can do to improve your chances. Making a specific plan can help you to improve, and the motivational effect of taking positive action should not be underestimated.

Good luck!

Index

N

O

P

Q

R

S

T